ADOBE® CREATIVE SUITE 5
WEB PREMIUM
HOW-TOs

100 ESSENTIAL TECHNIQUES

DAVID KARLINS

Adobe Creative Suite 5 Web Premium How-Tos

100 Essential Techniques

David Karlins

This Adobe Press book is published by Peachpit.

Peachpit
1249 Eighth Street
Berkeley, CA 94710
510/524-2178
510/524-2221 (fax)

Peachpit is a division of Pearson Education.

For the latest on Adobe Press books, go to: www.adobepress.com

To report errors, please send a note to: errata@peachpit.com

Editor: Rebecca Gulick
Production Editor: Hilal Sala
Copyeditor: Liz Welch
Proofreader: Patricia Pane
Cover and Interior Designer: Mimi Heft
Indexer: Valerie Haynes Perry
Technical Reviewer: Bruce K. Hopkins
Compositor: codeMantra

ISBN-13: 978-0-321-71986-7

ISBN-10:   0-321-71986-7

9 8 7 6 5 4 3 2 1

Printed and bound in the United States of America

Acknowledgements

Thanks to the entire editorial and production staff who made this book possible, including Peachpit Senior Editor Rebecca Gulick, who oversaw the whole operation. A tip of the hat to Victor Gavenda, Executive Editor, Adobe Press, for his critical input. Thanks also to Liz Welch, for a yeowoman editing job. Technical editor Bruce K. Hopkins served as guru of consult and vigilant fact-checker. Production Editor Hilal Sala accommodated my picky requests for layout tweaks. Special appreciation goes to Eric D. Geist for permission to use his jewelry as models for Web projects in this book. And, finally, thanks to my students, readers, and clients who asked hard questions, posed frustrating problems, refused to take no for an answer on their design concepts, and provided the raw material for the approach and content in this book.

Contents

CHAPTER ONE

Creating a Web Site in Dreamweaver CS5

The topics in this book are not sequential—you can dive in wherever you need to, work backward, or jump around. But if you're approaching the whole process of creating a Web site with Adobe Creative Suite 5, it makes sense to start with Dreamweaver. Dreamweaver functions as the coordinating center for Web sites. A good grasp of Dreamweaver is helpful to seeing the big picture of how other elements of your site fit together.

When you create a Web site with Adobe CS5, Dreamweaver plays the role of the orchestra conductor. Dreamweaver organizes and presents photos prepared in Adobe Photoshop CS5…artwork from Adobe Illustrator CS5…animation from Flash Professional CS5…interactive elements from Flash Catalyst CS5…video compressed for the Web using Adobe Media Encoder CS5…and more.

We'll explore *all* these tools in this book—in enough depth for you to create a professional-quality, inviting, cutting-edge Web site. But we'll start with Dreamweaver. The core of a Dreamweaver Web site is what Dreamweaver defines as a *site*. *Web site* is a generic term for—well, a Web site, but in Dreamweaver, the term has a specific meaning: a set of files grouped together in a folder that is controlled exclusively by Dreamweaver.

Define a Web site *before* you create Web pages or add content elements (like images or media). When you do that, Dreamweaver connects your Web pages to each other with links. It ensures images and media are properly embedded in pages. When you move or rename a Web page (or any file in your site), Dreamweaver updates any links that are affected by that change. And your Dreamweaver Web site can manage (usually one, but sometimes more) style sheet files that control the formatting of multiple pages across a site.

Defining a Dreamweaver Web site is also necessary when you get ready to transfer your site content from your local computer to a remote server, where others can access your content.

This chapter starts by walking you through the process of defining both a local (on your own computer) and a remote (on a server) Web site. The bulk of the chapter walks you through the basic process of creating Web-page content. The next chapter in this book will explore the process of laying out and formatting that content.

#1 Defining a Local Web Site

Dreamweaver CS5 has simplified the process of creating a Dreamweaver site. Previous versions of Dreamweaver tried to compel you to define a remote site (on a Web server) at the same time you created a local site (on your own computer). But the reality is that many people create a local site before they are sure where their remote site will be hosted, and so this simplified site definition process is welcome.

The essence of preparing to create a Dreamweaver site is to choose a folder on your computer that will store *all* the elements of the site. If you have a bunch of content already that you want to include in your site, a good way to start is by copying that content from the Web, from your flash drives, and from your hard drive, all into *one* folder on your computer.

Identify Your Audience

Media-rich sites require high-bandwidth (fast) connections. Using Flash requires that visitors have the Flash Player installed (which is not available on the iPhone, iPod Touch, or iPad).

Follow these steps to define a local site in Dreamweaver:

1. Collect your entire site content in a single folder. You can create sub-folders (subdirectories) for images, media, Web pages, and so on. But all these folders must be within the folder that will serve as your local site folder.

2. Launch Dreamweaver CS5. From the Document window menu, choose Site > New Site. The Site Definition dialog opens.

3. With Site selected in the category list on the left side of the dialog, enter a name for your site. This is just a name for your own reference; it can contain spaces, upper- and lowercase characters, special symbols, or anything else that helps you remember what site you are working on.

Planning a Site

In this compressed guide to the *essentials* of setting up a Web site with Adobe Creative Suite 5, I can only address issues of content and aesthetics in the most compressed way. Sidebars in this section will give advice on the three key aspects of planning a site: content, aesthetic theme, and audience.

Plan Site Content

A typical approach is to draw "wireframes," page layouts that eschew aesthetic elements like color schemes, fonts, and graphics but identify what content will go on what page. Creating a set of wireframes, even if simple sketches, will help identify issues you need to address in terms of what content should be emphasized on your site, what content should be secondary, and what content should be available but not prominent. There are sections in both the Photoshop and Illustrator chapters of this book that document how to create wireframes in those programs. Or just use the back of some recycled paper and sketch out wireframes by hand.

4. Click the Browse for Folder icon to the right of the Local Site Folder field (**Figure 1**), and browse to and select the folder into which you copied content that will be used in your Web site (in step 1).

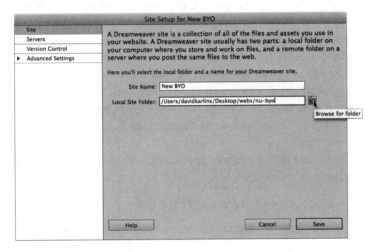

Figure 1 Defining a local site.

5. Expand the Advanced Settings options in the categories list and select the Local Info tab. If you want Dreamweaver to automatically save images to one folder on your local storage system (usually a hard drive), you can navigate to a folder using the folder icon next to the "Default images folder" field. This is not a particularly essential option, and it can get in your way if you want to manually control where your files are stored.

6. Choose the "Links relative to Document" option. This is the most efficient and reliable way to generate and update links between files and to define links for embedded images.

7. Select the Enable cache check box. This activates the Assets panel that displays all site content. You may or may not use the Assets panel to track your content, but with this check box selected, you have that option.

8. With your local site defined, click Save. Dreamweaver will now organize your files into a Dreamweaver site.

Develop a *Basic* Aesthetic Theme

Design images that will serve as banners or navigation icons. Choose a color scheme (you can Google for "Web color schemes" for inspiration). And think about what font sizes and colors you like (scope out other sites you like for ideas).

But I'm a Designer

"I'm a designer, not a file manager!" I hear you. Organizing files and defining a site is not my favorite part of Web design either. But think ahead: Web sites, especially the latest generation of Web sites, involve a *lot* of files. In addition to the HTML file that stores your basic content, Web pages often involve image files, media files, JavaScript files to control animation and interactivity, CSS (Cascading Style Sheet) files to control formatting, and more! Fortunately, Dreamweaver handles all the work of ensuring that these files are linked properly, work together, and can be easily transferred from your local computer to a remote server—*as long as* you define and work within a Dreamweaver site.

#2 Connecting to a Remote Site

What You Need from a Web Host

When you obtain a remote server, make sure the provider gives you the following information:

- The FTP address
- Your login name
- Your password

Most developers create and test their Web pages first on their own computer, and then upload that content to a remote server once it has been tested, proofread, vetted and approved, and deemed ready to share. This is a different process, for example, than working with a blog site, where content is composed and submitted directly to a server. The two-stage development process in Dreamweaver allows you to thoroughly test your site before going live.

You don't need a remote site until you are ready to go live. And feel free to skip this topic for now if you are only working on a local site. But when you *are* ready to upload your site, you will need to purchase a Web-hosting server. Web-site hosting costs as little as $5/month, sometimes for unlimited server space (file size) and bandwidth (amount of content flowing to and from your site). Shop around—if you do not have a remote site, there are many vendors ready to sell you one.

To define a remote site, follow these steps:

1. Choose Site > Manage Sites to open the Manage Sites dialog.

2. Click on your site (if more than one are listed), and click the Edit button. The Site Setup dialog for your site opens.

3. Select Servers from the categories on the left side of the dialog. Click the Add New Server "+" button in the lower-left corner of the server list area. The Site Setup dialog appears.

4. In the Basic tab of the Servers category dialog, choose FTP from the Connect Using drop-down menu. This is how almost all remote sites connect with your computer to transfer files (FTP stands for File Transfer Protocol). If your hosting company gave you other instructions (like logging in as SFTP, *Secure* FTP), follow those directions.

5. On the Basic tab of the Site Setup dialog, enter a name for your server. This can be anything that helps you remember the server if you are using a lot of different servers (which is unlikely, meaning you can pretty much type any old thing in this field).

6. In the FTP host field, enter the FTP location provided by your Web-host provider.

7. In the Username field, enter the login or username provided by your Web-host provider.

8. In the Password field, enter the password provided by your Web-host provider.

9. In the Root Directory field, enter a root directory *only if your Web-hosting service supplied you with one and indicated it was required.*

10. In the Web URL field, enter the URL for your Web site. This is different than the FTP address used to transfer files with Dreamweaver. Instead, here you enter the (Web-site address) for your new Web site, typically starting with http://.

11. Expand the More Options section of the dialog. If your Web-host provider allows you to connect using passive FTP, select the "Use passive FTP" check box. You can try connecting to your site without this check box selected, and then try enabling passive FTP if your connection fails.

12. If you are working behind a firewall, your system administrator might need to configure the Proxy Host settings in the Site Definition dialog. However, normally Dreamweaver adopts the same firewall settings you use with other programs to connect to the Internet, so custom settings are not necessary.

13. Select the FTP Performance Optimization check box to speed up file transfers.

(continued on next page)

Passwords Are Case Sensitive

Password and login information is case sensitive and must be entered exactly as provided. Once you have entered an FTP location, a login, and a password, you have defined the essentials of your connection.

14. After you define the remote connection, click the Test button. If your connection works, the confirmation dialog appears (**Figure 2a**).

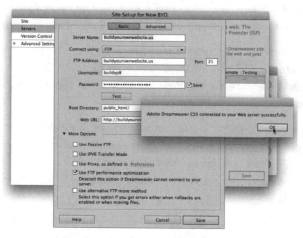

Figure 2a Testing a server connection.

Additional server parameters are defined on the Advanced tab of the Site Setup dialog. Let's briefly survey them:

1. Select the Advanced tab to view new settings.

2. Keep the Maintain Synchronization Information check box selected; this enables powerful tools for synchronizing your local and remote sites.

3. Leave other options unchecked. The Automatically Upload Files to Server on Save bypasses the normal two-step process of testing your site locally before uploading it to the world. The checkout options are for complex sites with teams of designers. The Testing Server is for live data sites where you are creating connections to server-side scripts that enable live data from databases.

Note
Connecting to live server-side databases is beyond the scope of this book. Those connections can be defined by a team of database programmers, or created more simply using a content management system (CMS) like Drupal.

4. After you define Advanced settings for your remote server, click Save (**Figure 2b**).

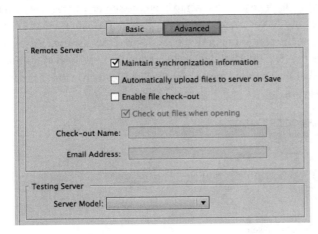

Figure 2b Advanced server connection settings.

You have now defined both your local and remote sites, and Dreamweaver can manage synchronizing the two.

#3 Managing Sites in the Files Panel

No File Management During File Transfer

Although you can edit Web pages while files transfer to (or from) a remote server, you cannot do other file management activities on the server while files are in transit. This means, for example, that you cannot edit your site in the Site Definition dialog while you are transferring files. But you can open a Web page on your local site and edit it.

Coordinating Local and Remote Sites

As a general rule, avoid editing filenames, folder locations, and so on at your remote server. If you stick to a protocol of creating and managing files on your local site, and then transferring those files to the remote site, you'll ensure that both sites match—what you see on your local site will match what visitors see at your remote site.

The Dreamweaver Files panel provides tools for managing files at both the local *and* remote servers. That is a potentially scary power to have.

(continued on next page)

With a site open, you connect to your remote server by clicking the "Connects to remote host" icon in the Files panel (in either Expanded or Collapsed view). Once you connect to a remote server, you can see either local or remote server content using the View pop-up menu in the Files panel. To see the content of both the local and remote sites at the same time, click the "Expand to show local and remote sites" icon in the Files panel toolbar. In Expanded mode, click the Site Files icon in the Files panel toolbar (**Figure 3a**).

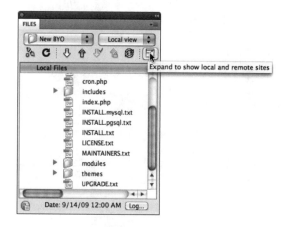

Figure 3a Expanding the Files panel.

To upload an entire site from your local folder to the remote server, follow these steps:

1. Click the root folder of your local site in the Files panel—either in Expanded or Collapsed view.

2. With the root folder selected, click the Put File(s) icon in the Files panel toolbar (**Figure 3b**).

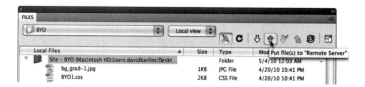

Figure 3b Uploading an entire Web site.

3. Dreamweaver will prompt you to confirm the action by clicking OK, and then it will upload your entire Web site. The Background File Activity dialog will track the progress of uploading your site.

Once you have uploaded your site, you won't want to waste time re-uploading the entire site each time you change a file. Instead, you can upload selected files. Shift-click or Ctrl-click/Command-click to select files in the Files panel, and choose Put to upload the selected files.

You can also upload open pages directly from the Document window. Do this by clicking the File Management tool in the Document toolbar and choosing Put (**Figure 3c**).

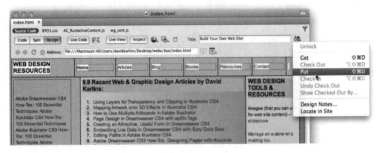

Figure 3c Uploading an open Web page.

You can synchronize either files you have selected (by Shift-clicking) in the Files window or your entire site. And you can synchronize your site either by updating the server with newer files from the currently open local site, or vice versa (moving newer files from the server to your local computer).

To synchronize your local and remote sites, follow these steps:

1. From the main Dreamweaver menu, choose Site > Synchronize Sitewide. The Synchronize Files dialog appears.

2. From the Synchronize pop-up menu in the Synchronize Files dialog, choose either selected files or the whole site.

(continued on next page)

It means that you can rename, move, and delete files from your remote server and, in the process, corrupt your remote server files so they no longer match the files on your local server. This is part of the reason why standard procedure is to edit files on a local site before uploading to a server.

Downloading Files

In addition to putting (uploading) files to your server, you can download files from your server. If you are the only person working on a Web site (the only person who places files on the server in Dreamweaver), you will rarely need to transfer files from the remote server to your local computer. Because all files originate on your local computer, you can overwrite files on the server by uploading the matching file from your local computer. However, if you are working with other developers on a site, you might need to download a file that was updated by someone else. In that case, click the file in the server, and then click the Get File(s) icon in the Files panel toolbar.

What Are Dependent Files?

If you transfer a Web page with an embedded image to a remote server, a dialog opens asking if you want to also upload *dependent files*. These are files that open along with the page. An embedded image, for example, appears when a page is opened in a browser. The page won't work correctly without the photo being uploaded to the server along with the page. Therefore, you need to include dependent files if you are uploading a page with an image. The next time you upload that page, however, you do not need to re-upload the image file unless you have changed it.

Other files that Dreamweaver considers dependent are style sheets that define how a page looks. Embedded media files are also considered dependent files.

What is *not* considered a dependent file is any page or other file to which that page is *linked*. For instance, if you upload a page that links to another page,

(continued on next page)

3. In the Direction pop-up menu, choose from the options—"get from server," "put to server," or both—that allow you to transfer files from local site to server, server to local site, or both ways, replacing older files with more recent ones.

4. In the Synchronize Files dialog, click the Preview button. Dreamweaver connects to your remote site and creates a list of files that meet your criteria ("new at the remote site," "newer at the local site," or both). The list is displayed in a dialog (again) called Synchronize. Click OK, and Dreamweaver will update all files according to the criteria you defined.

A couple other icons to note in the Files panel: The Connect icon connects the Files window to your remote site. The Refresh icon refreshes local and remote site views.

When it's time for housekeeping and moving files from one folder to another, you can also rely on the Dreamweaver Files panel. You can display the Files panel by choosing Window > Files or by pressing Shift+Command+F (Mac) or the F8 function key (Windows) to toggle between displaying and hiding the Files panel.

The Files panel menu has options for typical file management actions, like creating new files or folders, renaming files, copying or pasting files, deleting files, and so on.

The basic rule for working with files is this: *Never* change filenames or move files between folders using your operating system's file management tools. Instead, *always* rely on Dreamweaver's Files panel to manage filenames and to move files between folders.

The Site folder looks and works like the Finder (for Mac) and Windows Explorer (for Windows) utilities. It allows you to drag files between folders, copy and paste files, rename files, and delete files, just as you would do in Finder or Explorer.

When you define your local Web site in Dreamweaver, you define a local site folder. Dreamweaver knows that this folder is where all your site files *should be* kept. If you open a file from another folder or copy or move a file from another folder, Dreamweaver will prompt you to save a copy of that file in your Web folder. For example, if you embed an image in a Web page, Dreamweaver will prompt you to save that image to your site root or image folder when you place it on the page.

Index.htm or Index.html Is Your Home Page

Different servers have different rules for home pages, but generally the index.htm or index.html file serves as a Web-site home page. The home page is the file that opens when a visitor comes to your site. This has more significance when your site is transferred to a remote server and made accessible to visitors. But even when you are only working with a local site, defining a home page is necessary to generate a site map or prototype navigation links using the Dreamweaver Files panel.

you *still need to manually upload* the page to which the uploaded page is linked (if the linked page is missing or has been changed).

Why Use Dreamweaver's Files Panel for File Management?

You *could* delete, rename, or copy files that are part of your Dreamweaver site by using your operating system's file management tools. But don't. In a Web site, files are almost always connected to other files. You might have an image embedded in a page. If you change the name of that image file or move it to another folder, the link between that image and the page in which it is embedded becomes corrupted.

If you do all your file management in Dreamweaver, Dreamweaver will *fix* the problems caused by moving or renaming a file by redefining links that involve that file. For instance, if files in your Web site contain links to a file and that filename is changed, Dreamweaver will prompt you to change those links in an Update Files dialog.

#4 Creating and Saving Web Pages

When you choose File > New, the New Document dialog opens. Throughout this book you will explore some of the most useful categories of new documents, but the first and main type of new document you'll create in the New Document dialog is a basic page. The basic and main type of Web page you'll create is an HTML page (**Figure 4a**).

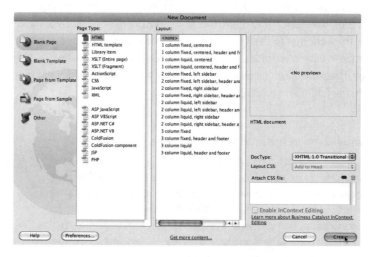

Figure 4a New Document dialog with a new HTML Web page selected.

Clicking the Create button in the New Document dialog generates a new page and opens that page in the Document window. The Document window is where you design Web pages. In the Document window, you can open many pages at a time and edit them. You use the Document window to create or paste text, embed images, define links, place and sometimes create page elements like style sheets (that control the look of a page), input forms, embed animation, and create interactive objects (that react to actions by a visitor).

You work in the Document window when you open an existing Web page or when you create a new one. Use the File menu to open an existing Web page (File > Open or File > Open Recent to access a list of recently opened pages) or to create a new Web page (File > New).

The right side of the status bar (at the bottom of the Document window) has some handy tools that aid in design techniques. The Select and Hand tools provide two ways to navigate around your document.

Changing Units of Measurement

You can adjust the units displayed for window size or the connection speed used to estimate download time in the Status Bar category in the Preferences dialog. On the Mac, choose Dreamweaver > Preferences and in Windows choose Edit > Preferences, and then select the Status Bar category to edit these parameters.

Choosing a Document Type Definition (DTD)

From the far-left column in the New Document dialog, choose Blank Page. From the Page Type list, choose HTML. In the Layout column, select <none>. In the Doc-Type (Document Type; DTD) field, choose the default document type, XHTML 1.0 Transitional.

(continued on next page)

Creating a Web Site in Dreamweaver CS5

The Select tool is the default mode; it allows you to click on objects or click and drag to select text. The Hand tool works like similar tools in Adobe Photoshop or Illustrator, allowing you to grab a section of the page and drag it in or out of view.

- The Zoom tool is used to draw a marquee and enlarge a section of a page.

- To exit either the Zoom or Hand tool mode and return to the default cursor, click the Select tool.

- The Set Magnification drop-down menu is another way to define magnification.

- The Window size display indicates the size of your Design window, normally in pixels.

- The File Size/Download Time display estimates download time for the page parameters (**Figure 4b**).

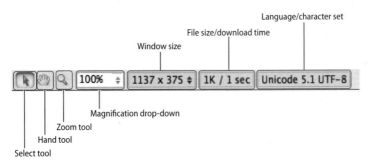

Figure 4b Status bar tools.

After you create a new page, you need to *save* it with a *filename,* and you need to assign a page *title* to that page. Every Web page needs a filename and a title. The filename is mainly an internal element. It is used to locate the file in a Web site and to link the file to other files. As such, filenames don't have to be very creative, but they should avoid special characters like commas, ampersands (&), percent signs (%), spaces, and so on. You'll be safe if you stick to lowercase alphanumeric characters, plus the helpful dash (-) and underscore (_) characters.

Then click Create to generate a new Web page.

Dreamweaver CS5 uses XHTML 1.0 Transitional as the default document type for HTML Web pages. By generating XHTML-compatible coding for your Web page, you allow your Web page to integrate cutting-edge dynamic data content—content that is updated at a remote source and embedded (updated) in your Web page. Such dynamic data systems are issues that are decided at systemwide levels, not by a Web-page designer. But by accepting Dreamweaver's default document type of XHTML 1.0 Transitional, you embed the ability to interact with and display dynamic data at any stage of system development.

Page Filename and Page Title

Every Web page has both a filename and a page title. The *filename* is the way the file is identified and located within a Web site. Page *titles* describe the page content for visitors. They *can* contain special characters, including punctuation and spaces.

There is a special requirement for filenames assigned to a site home page. A site home page is the page that opens when visitors enter your URL in the address bar of their browser. This URL does not specify a file but only a server location. Once the server location is open in a browser, browsers detect the home page by looking for a file named index.htm or index.html. *Never* create files named both index.htm and index.html; this will confuse your server, the browsers, and you. Instead, choose one or the other, and create a file called index.html (or index.htm). This will be your home page.

Page titles are different from page filenames. Titles have nothing to do with how files are saved, linked to, or managed at a server. Therefore, they can contain any characters, including special characters like commas and other punctuation marks. As noted, *every* page has a page title, but unless you assign a page title, the default "Untitled Page" page title appears in browser title bars.

You can enter (or change) page title information in the Title field in the Document toolbar. If the Document toolbar is not visible in the Document window, choose View > Toolbars > Document (**Figure 4c**).

Title: Site Building Resources

Figure 4c Entering a page title.

#5 Working with Text and Defining Links

There are two basic options for bringing text to a Web page:

- Copying relatively unformatted text into Dreamweaver and formatting it in Dreamweaver

- Using export tools in your word processor and import tools in Dreamweaver to translate the markup language from PostScript to HTML

If you copy and paste text from your word processor into Dreamweaver, you can still use the formatting tools provided by Dreamweaver. These tools are designed to apply formatting that can be interpreted well and consistently by browsers. The downside of this method is that you need to reapply formatting in Dreamweaver.

On the other hand, saving your word processing file as an HTML file (some word processors have a Save As Web Page option) allows you to bring as much formatting as possible with the text as you move it into Dreamweaver. The downside of this method is that the formatting generated by your word processor is unlikely to hold up as consistently in browsers as text formatted in Dreamweaver.

If you save a Word file as an HTML page or if you import a Word file into a Dreamweaver Web page, you can clean up the HTML that results by choosing Commands > Clean Up Word HTML. From the Clean Up HTML pop-up menu, choose a version of Word. Then accept the default checkbox settings. Doing this will strip from the generated HTML any coding that would confuse browsers (**Figure 5a**).

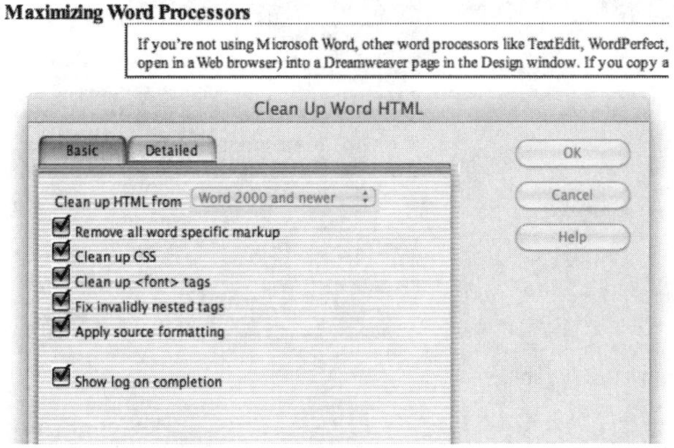

Figure 5a Cleaning up imported HTML code.

Maximizing Word Processors

If you're not using Microsoft Word, other word processors like TextEdit, WordPerfect, and OpenOffice all save to Word format. Or, you can copy and paste text from any source (including a Web page that is open in a Web browser) into a Dreamweaver page in the Design window. If you copy and paste, you will lose most or all of your formatting.

Importing Spreadsheets and Word Documents in Dreamweaver CS5 for Windows

The Windows version of Dreamweaver allows you to import Microsoft Word (and Excel) files directly to Web pages. This saves the step of opening the file in a word processor and saving it as an HTML file. To import a Word or Excel file, open the Web page to which you are importing the file, and choose File > Import > Word Document (or Excel Document). The Import Document dialog opens, and you can choose a few options for importing, ranging from Text Only (no formatting) to Text with Structure Plus Full Formatting (which retains the most formatting).

Two Types of Links

Generally speaking, link targets can be one of two types: relative (internal to your site) or absolute (outside your site).

(continued on next page)

Links are one of the most basic and dynamic elements of a Web page. In fact, hypertext, the H in HTML, refers to text that could have link properties (at least at the time the name was coined). Links can be associated with text or images.

The easiest way to define links is to use the Properties inspector (choose Window > Properties if the inspector is not displaying). To define an absolute link, start by selecting the text you want to link from. In the Properties inspector, click the HTML button if that is not selected (deselect the CSS button). With the text selected, you can type an absolute link in the Link box in the Properties inspector (**Figure 5b**).

Figure 5b Entering an absolute-link target for selected text.

To define a relative link, with the link text selected, click the blue Browse for File icon next to the Link box in the Properties inspector. The Select File dialog opens. Navigate to the linked file, and click Choose to generate a link to that file. The relative link appears in the Link box in the Properties inspector (**Figure 5c**).

Figure 5c Defining a relative link.

The other attribute that is important to define for a link is the Target window. By default, links open in the *same* browser window as the linking page, causing the linking page to disappear. Visitors can click the Back button on their browser to return to the original, linking page.

If you want a page to open in a *new* browser window, go to the Properties inspector and choose the _blank attribute in the Target pop-up menu (**Figure 5d**).

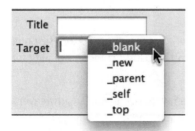

Figure 5d Defining the _blank link target that will open the link in a new browser window.

Both are defined in the Properties inspector for selected text (or a selected image).

Relative Links

With relative links, you don't define where the link is found on the Internet; you define where the link is located relative to the current page—and at your Web site.

Email Links

To convert text with an email address into an email link, simply select the text and choose Insert > Email Link. The Email Link dialog appears, and the text you selected is automatically identified as the email link. Or, you can select any text (or image) and define that as an email link. To do so, first select the text or image that will serve as the email link. Then choose Insert > Email Link. The Email Link dialog appears. If you selected text as an email link, that text appears in the Text box in the Email Link dialog. Type the email address for the link into the EMail box.

#6 Embedding and Editing Images

You embed photos or other images in Web pages with Dreamweaver. But try to avoid using Dreamweaver as your image-editing tool. Dreamweaver CS5 does come with a few, very minimalist and rather primitive image-editing tools. But programs (Adobe Photoshop and Photoshop Elements among the most prominent) allow you to export image files to JPEG, GIF, or PNG format, and resize and reformat images to look better and download faster on the Web.

That said, there are two basic approaches to embedding images in Dreamweaver:

- Prepare the image in Photoshop (or another image editor), sizing it, choosing a Web-friendly format, and adjusting color and quality for the Web.

- Copy and paste the image into Dreamweaver, and use Dreamweaver's limited but functional tools to apply appropriate Web image settings.

Let's walk through both of these options, starting with an image that has been saved to a JPEG, GIF, or PNG (pronounced "ping") format. The image should be in your Dreamweaver Site folder (refer to #1, "Defining a Local Web Site"). To embed an image that has already been saved and resized, follow these steps:

1. With your cursor at the insertion point for the photo (this should generally be at the *beginning* of a paragraph if there is text on the page), choose Insert > Image. In the Select Image Source dialog (**Figure 6a**), navigate to the image that you saved to your Site folder (a quick shortcut is to click the Site Root button in the dialog to jump to your Dreamweaver Site folder).

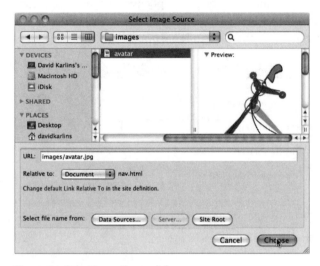

Figure 6a Select Image Source dialog.

2. Select the image you wish to insert and click Choose.

(continued on next page)

3. With default settings for accessibility (these can be edited in the Preferences dialog—choose Edit > Preferences in Windows or Dreamweaver > Preferences on a Mac), you will be prompted to enter Image Tag Accessibility Attributes. Entering a brief description of the image in the Alternate Text box provides alternate content for visitors to your site who cannot see, or who have images disabled in their browsing environment. If long descriptions of images are appropriate, they can be saved as separate Web pages, and linked to in the Long Description box in the dialog (**Figure 6b**).

Figure 6b Defining alternate text for an image.

4. When you click OK in the Image Tag Accessibility Attributes dialog, the image appears on the page.

Even though you prepared this image in a program like Photoshop, you may want to edit the appearance in Dreamweaver, including by aligning the image to flow text around it. I'll show you how to do that shortly, but first, let's examine the other main scenario for bringing illustrations into Dreamweaver:

To copy and paste an image into Dreamweaver, follow these steps.

1. Copy the image into your operating system clipboard. To copy an image from the Web, select the image in a Web browser and choose Copy Image from the Control-click (Mac) or right-click (Windows) context menu. Or, in other programs, choose Edit > Copy.

2. Click in Dreamweaver at the point where you want to insert the image, and choose Edit > Paste. Depending on the source of the image and the image file type, Dreamweaver will immediately prompt you with either the Image Description (Alt Text) dialog or the Image Preview window.

3. If the Image Preview window opens, use the Format drop-down menu to choose a format (usually JPEG works best for photos). Use the Quality slider to define image quality (better color accuracy). Better image quality means a larger image, which will take longer to download. Select the Progressive check box for JPEGs, or the Interlacing check box for PNG and GIF format so that the image will "fade in" while it downloads, as opposed to appearing as line-by-line pixels starting at the top of the image.

4. You can experiment with other image settings, like format, quality, and the sharpen Color Edges check box by choosing the 2-up or 4-up displays (the last two options in the row of tools at the bottom of the Image Preview dialog). Choose a panel and apply settings. Note the quality of the image, and the file size and download time (**Figure 6c**).

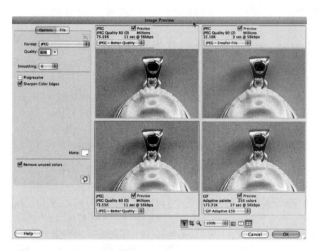

Figure 6c Comparing different file formats and settings for an image for the Web in Dreamweaver's Image Preview window.

5. When you have defined settings, be sure you have the correct version of your image selected in the 2-up or 4-up display, and click OK.

(continued on next page)

Online Image Formats

- **JPEG** images support millions of colors and are best for photographs. *Progressive* JPEG files "fade in" as they download rather than appearing line by line.

- **GIF** images support far fewer colors than the JPEG format and are not usually used for photos. But GIF images support *transparency*, which allows the background of a Web page to show through empty spots in the image. GIF images can be defined as *interlaced*. Interlacing, like the progressive attribute in JPEG images, allows the image to fade in as it downloads.

(continued on next page)

The Save Web Image dialog appears. Click the Site Root button to jump to your Dreamweaver Site folder, and enter a filename in the Save As box. Then click Save.

6. Enter a brief description of the image in the Image Description (Alt Text) box for visitors to your site who cannot see, or who have images disabled in their browsing environment. Click OK to place the image.

Differences Between Print and Web Images

Preparing images for the Web presents a separate set of challenges than preparing images for print. There are several major differences between images on the Web and images prepared for print documents. These differences include these parameters:

- With the rapid development of new mobile and large-screen devices and monitors, *resolution* (dots per inch, or dpi) varies considerably, but in general, Web images will be displayed at a much lower resolution than print images. Web images are usually saved at 72 or 96 dpi, whereas print images are routinely saved at 300 dpi and higher resolution.

- Web images are saved using the RGB (Red, Green, Blue) color system, whereas print images usually use CMYK (Cyan, Magenta, Yellow, Black) color mode.

- Web images are saved to JPEG, GIF, or PNG format, whereas print images are often saved in the TIFF format.

Using Photoshop to Prepare Photos for the Web

Images that have a small file size and fast downloading time (and are therefore typically low-quality) are generated using compression. Compression "looks for" pixels in an image that do not need to be saved as part of the file information, and it reduces file size by saving less of the image definition. You'll have the most control over image compression using a program like Photoshop. See Chapter 8, "Preparing Photos for the Web with Photoshop," for an in-depth look.

Once you've embedded an image in a Web page, you can use image-editing and alignment tools in the Properties inspector to control how

- Add spacing around the image by entering values (in pixels) in the V (vertical) Space or H (horizontal) Space boxes.

- Align an image (flow text to the right or left) by choosing right or left in the Align drop-down menu (**Figure 6d**).

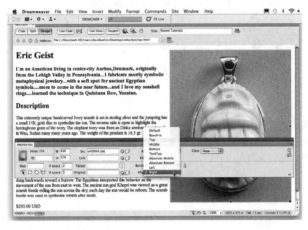

Figure 6d A right-aligned image with 2 pixels of vertical spacing and 5 pixels of horizontal spacing.

- Resize an image by selecting it, and clicking and dragging on a handle. Normally, you'll want to Shift+click on the lower-right resizing handle to maintain the height-to-width ratio of the original image (so you don't distort it). After you resize an image, you can click the Resample button in the Properties inspector to reduce the file size for a resized image.

(continued on next page)

(continued on next page)

- **PNG** images support more colors, like JPEG, and allow you to define a transparent color, like GIF files. However, PNG format is generally not acceptable for photos because it lacks the JPEG format's capacity to manage colors and photo detail.

Images Can Be Resized Smaller, Not Bigger in Dreamweaver

When you resize and resample images in Dreamweaver, you can make them smaller but not bigger. Increasing the size of an image, without adding pixels, will make the image grainy and distorted. You *can* resize images and add pixels to maintain image quality in programs like Photoshop, but not in Dreamweaver.

- Use the Crop, Contrast, and Sharpen tools in the Dreamweaver Properties inspector to do very basic photo editing. When you select the Crop tool, with an image selected, movable crop marks appear. Click the Crop tool again to crop the image. The Brightness and Contrast button opens a small dialog with interactive Brightness and Contrast sliders (use the Preview check box to see the effect of your changes on the image). The Sharpen tool opens a one-slider dialog that allows you to apply a Sharpen effect and preview it (**Figure 6e**).

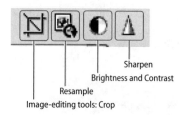

Sharpen

Brightness and Contrast

Resample

Image-editing tools: Crop

Figure 6e Resizing an image and identifying image-editing tools.

#7 Inspecting Code

The Dreamweaver CS5 window has three views: Code, Design, and Split. Code view displays *only* code and is used by designers who want to bypass Dreamweaver's ability to generate code. Design view hides most code, providing a graphical design interface. Split view displays code on the left (normally) of the Document window and a graphical design environment on the right (**Figure 7a**).

Figure 7a Viewing a page in Split view.

   To toggle between views, choose one of the three view buttons on the left side of the Document toolbar (if that toolbar is not visible, choose View > Toolbars > Document).

   You can create complex, appealing, and high-end Web sites using Dreamweaver, and the rest of the CS5 Web suite, *without* resorting to any kind of coding. That said, you can *also* easily access coding in Dreamweaver, and you can use Dreamweaver CS5's handy new Inspect button to easily associate code with elements in the Design window.

   When you click the Inspect button, Dreamweaver prompts you to click a Switch Now link just under the toolbar. Doing so switches your display to Split view if it is set to Design or Code view, and automatically enables Live View and Live Code, which converts your Design window into something like a browser window (see #8, "Previewing in Live View and Browsers" for more on Live View). If you click the Switch Now link, you also display the CSS Styles panel, a powerful panel for controlling Web and page layout and format, and one you'll begin to explore in Chapters 2

Advantages to Split View

There are a number of advantages to working in Split view, both for designers who know how to write code, as well as for designers who are not comfortable or proficient in writing their own code. Split view is a way for proficient coders to see a graphical representation of the code they are writing. And Split view is a good way for designers who are not conversant in coding to become familiar with coding, since generated code appears as you create elements in the graphical design window. Even though Dreamweaver is the best existing program for generating HTML and other page-layout code, there are times when the only way to troubleshoot a design problem is to edit the code directly. If you edit code in Split view, you can see the effect by clicking in the Design (WYSIWYG) window.

and 3 of this book. For now, the CSS Styles panel is not essential, but Split view and Live View are, because the point of the Inspect button is to help you examine elements of your page in a browser-like environment, and link them to associated code.

With Inspect mode on, select any element of your page. The code associated with that element is highlighted in the Code side of Split view. Use this feature either to learn coding, or to identify code and edit it directly in Split or Code view (**Figure 7b**).

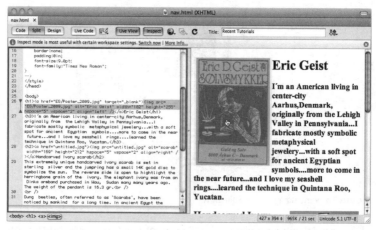

Figure 7b Inspecting code for an image.

The Live Code button in the Document toolbar must be deselected in order to edit code. With Code view in one window and Live view in another, you can edit code. You can then click the Refresh Design View icon in the Document toolbar to see your edited code reflected in Live view, where you can test it in a browser.

#8 Previewing in Live View and Browsers

Dreamweaver CS5 provides at least four ways to test your Web page in a viewing environment. The most substantial of these is new to CS5: Adobe BrowserLab. You can also preview pages in a browser installed on your own computer (BrowserLab gives you access to all major browsers, whether or not they are installed on your computer). You can also preview pages in Live view. Finally, you can see how your page will look on a mobile device in Device Central.

The first time you use BrowserLab, you'll be prompted to sign up with Adobe to use it. As of this writing, BrowserLab is free, and we hope it will stay that way. After you sign up for BrowserLab, choose File > Preview in Browser > Adobe BrowserLab, or open the BrowserLab panel (Windows > Extensions > Adobe BrowserLab). In BrowserLab, you can choose 1-up (one browser view at a time) or 2-up, which is convenient for comparing your page in two different browsers. Use the drop-down menu to preview your page in any browser (**Figure 8a**).

Figure 8a Previewing a Web page in two different browsers at the same time at Adobe BrowserLab.

Dreamweaver CS5's Live view allows you to *test* pages in Design view. For example, in Live view links work like links—you can click them and follow them. With Live view turned off, when you click on a text link you can't follow the link (unless you Control-click (Mac) or right-click (Windows) and select Follow Link from the context menu), but you *can* edit the link text.

If you don't have access to BrowserLab, you can preview pages in browsers installed on your own computer by choosing File > Preview in Browser and then selecting one of your installed browsers.

Live view is not as accurate as previewing in an actual browser, but it does give you a basic sense of how your page will look. To switch to Live view, click the Live View button in the Document toolbar (or choose View > Live View). In Live view, you can test links, enter data into forms, and generally interact with your Web page just as you would in a browser (**Figure 8b**).

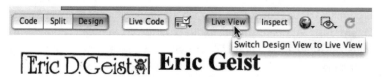

Figure 8b Toggling from Design view to Live view.

Additional controls over Live View display are available in the Browser Navigation toolbar (View > Toolbars > Browser Navigation). Options from the Live View Options drop-down menu in the Browser Navigation toolbar (**Figure 8c**) include defining whether links should function as links, along with rather complex options for controlling how JavaScript runs in Live view (for more on JavaScript in Dreamweaver, see Chapter 5, "Adding Effects and Interactivity with Spry and JavaScript").

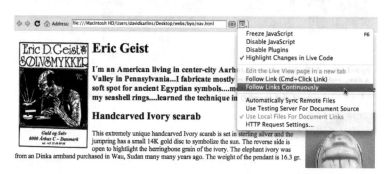

Figure 8c Live View options.

To preview your page in a mobile device, choose File > Preview in Browser > Device Central. You can preview your page in one of the versions of Flash for mobile devices (like Flash Player 10.1). Or you can click the Home icon in the Device Central Device Library and choose any of dozens of mobile devices to test your page (**Figure 8d**).

Figure 8d Previewing a Web page on a mobile device in Device Central.

Troubleshooting Preview in Device Central

If Dreamweaver detects that the page you are previewing in Device Central *might* be a page that will display live data from a server database, it will balk at previewing the page in Device Central until and unless a valid connection is defined to the remote server. As the scope of this book (with the exception of the Drupal and Dreamweaver exploration in Chapter 3) is sites that are not using live data, make sure that your Web page is saved as an HTML page (with an .html or .htm filename extension) and that you haven't selected the Testing check box in the Servers category of the Site Setup dialog.

CHAPTER TWO

Designing Web Pages in Dreamweaver with CSS Styles

Between Dreamweaver CS5 and CSS (Cascading Style Sheets), you can create Web-page designs much as you would design a print page in InDesign, wireframe (draw a rough mockup of a page) in Illustrator or Photoshop, or even draw a sketch of a page on a scratch pad.

And by saving all your CSS in an *external* style sheet file, all your formatting can be controlled by a single or a small number of style sheets. This makes it easy to manage page layout and design *sitewide*. When you change a style in an external style sheet, be it a page design (which we'll explore in this chapter) or other elements like the page and image format (which we'll explore in Chapter 3), you update the *entire site*.

External style sheets, by the way, are the basic element of content management system (CMS) themes. So you can use Dreamweaver's CSS tools to format Web pages generated by CMS applications like Drupal, WordPress, and Joomla! We'll explore that process in detail in Chapter 3, but as we survey different CSS techniques, I'll include references to how they apply to CMS as we go.

Before diving into page layout with CSS, just a note on degraded techniques: In the evolution of Web design, before CSS was as developed and accessible as it is now, tables were used for page layout. There is no reason to use tables at this point for page layout except that they remain a part of our evolutionary past, and we've inherited a world with many existing sites that do use tables for page design. I can't justify an exploration of using tables for page design in this book, but I did cover this sufficiently in *Adobe Dreamweaver CS4 How-Tos: 100 Essential Techniques*. Using tables to organize data is explored in Chapter 5, "Adding Effects and Interactivity with Spry and JavaScript" (#29, "Creating a Spry Data Source Table").

#9 Using Design Tools (Grids, Zoom…)

Redefining Zero Points

You can redefine the horizontal and/or vertical zero points for the rulers. Do this by dragging the icon at the intersection of the horizontal and vertical rulers into the Document window. The point at which you release your mouse becomes the new zero point for the horizontal and vertical rulers. To reset the rulers' zero points, choose View > Rulers > Reset Origin.

Using Guides

To place a horizontal or vertical guide on the page, click and drag a ruler into the Document window. To edit the location of a guide, click and drag it. You can also double-click a guide to edit the guide location or unit of measurement. Guides can be locked to prevent accidental editing: Choose View > Guides > Lock Guides.

(continued on next page)

Before you start designing page layouts with CSS in Dreamweaver, avail yourself of useful layout tools in Dreamweaver's Design window. I'll introduce you here to tools like grids and zoom, and walk you through the process of creating a "960" layout—a 960-pixel-wide Web page divided into 16 columns that is used universally in designing pages for CMSs and has wider applicability to any page design using columns.

Dreamweaver CS5's rulers, guides, and gridlines display much like those in Illustrator, InDesign, and Photoshop. To display rulers in an open document, choose View > Rulers > Show. The Rulers submenu also allows you to choose pixels, inches, or centimeters. For example, to facilitate generating a "960" page grid, choose pixels (**Figure 9a**).

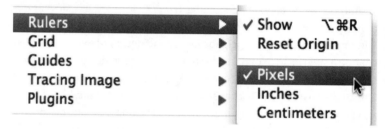

Figure 9a Choosing a pixels unit of measurement for rulers.

Grids are perhaps the most widely applicable layout tool in Dreamweaver. For example, to create a 960-pixel-wide page layout, you set the grid spacing at 60, making it easy to create 60-pixel-wide columns.

To display grids, choose View > Grid > Show Grid. To make grids magnetic, select View > Grid > Snap to Grid. Define grid properties by choosing View > Grid > Grid Settings. The Grid Settings dialog allows you to change the color of gridlines, spacing between grids, grid display and snap properties, and display (dots or lines). Click Apply to preview changes to the grid, or click OK to close the dialog and change grid settings in the Document window (**Figure 9b**).

Figure 9b Defining grid settings for working in a 960-pixel-wide page.

Rulers, Guides, and Grids: For Design Purposes Only

Rulers, guides, and grids do not actually become part of your Web page. They appear in the Document window (in Design view only) to help you place or align objects. Rulers, guides, and grids make it easy to define, size, and align page-layout elements. Regardless of which ruler, guide, or grid display you select in Dreamweaver, these elements *do not* display in a browser window.

Guides can also be made "magnetic" so that they either snap to objects on the page or objects on the page snap to them. To make a guide snap to elements on the page, choose View > Guides > Guides Snap to Elements. To make elements snap to guides, choose View > Guides > Snap to Guides. Clear guides by choosing View > Guides > Clear Guides.

What's with the 960 Grid?

The 960 grid has emerged as a widely used standard for Web-page design because a) it is a width supported by a wide range of viewing environments; and b) it is easily divisible into as many as 16 (60-pixel-wide) columns, providing a lot of flexibility in layout without designers having to resort to complicated math to divide a page into columns.

#10 Creating and Linking a Style Sheet

About the Body Tag

There are essentially two kind of CSS styles: ones that define attributes of HTML tags (the coding language used to define basic page layout), and ones that define other stuff—like containers that hold and position content. Of all tags, the Body tag is the most elemental. It defines all the basic attributes of a page, like margins, page background color, and fonts. In this How-To, you are learning to define all those basic page attributes in an external style sheet that can be applied to any page in your Web site.

The "control panel" for the look and feel of your Web site is the set of external style sheets (complex sites use more than one, but you can build a very inviting and robust design with a single style sheet).

The easiest way to generate a CSS file in Dreamweaver is to create a new style. As you do, you'll have the option of including that style in a new CSS file. In the following steps, you'll define a style and save it in a new style sheet and, in the process, create a style that defines the Body tag.

To define a new external CSS style sheet, with a Body tag that controls page margin, page background, and basic font appearance, follow these steps. They can be adapted to generate a CSS file using any tag as the initiating style.

1. In the Document window, click the New CSS Rule icon at the bottom of the CSS Styles panel (**Figure 10a**). The New CSS Rule dialog appears.

Figure 10a The New CSS Rule icon in the CSS Styles panel.

2. In the Selector Type area of the dialog, choose the type of style you want to define. To define the Body tag, choose Tag.

- Choose Class to apply formatting rules, which are independent of tags, to any selected text. If you are creating a Class style, enter a name for your style in the Name box.

- Choose ID to define a style that will apply to just one HTML tag.

- Choose Tag to define formatting for HTML elements, such as headings, paragraphs, images, tables, or pages. When the Tag radio button is selected, every HTML tag appears in a pull-down menu next to the Tag field.

- Choose Compound to define a style that will apply to everything you had selected in the Design window.

3. Choose (New Style Sheet File) from the Rule Definition pop-up menu to save the style you are defining to a new external style sheet (**Figure 10b**).

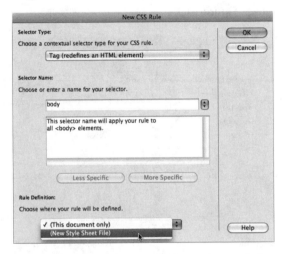

Figure 10b Generating a new style sheet with a new Body tag style.

4. Click OK in the New CSS Rule dialog. The Save Style Sheet File As dialog appears. This is a typical Save As dialog except that it automatically generates a CSS file with a .css file extension and translates any formatting you define into CSS coding. Navigate to the folder in which you want to save the style sheet and enter a filename in the Save As field. If you wish to use this and other How-Tos in this chapter as a recipe, assign the filename **newstyles.css**. Then click Save to generate the new CSS file.

(continued on next page)

5. After you click Save, the CSS Rule Definition dialog for the style you are defining opens. Different categories in the Category list offer formatting options for different kinds of page elements. We'll explore defining fonts in detail in Chapter 3, but you'll note now that you can define a global basic font family (a preferred font, along with substitutes if that font is not supported in a viewing environment), font size, color, and other attributes (**Figure 10c**).

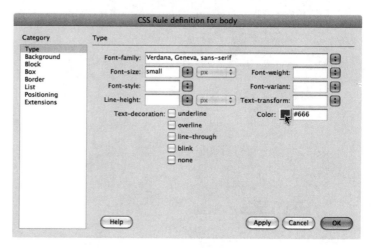

Figure 10c Defining a basic font style with the Body tag.

6. You can use the Background category to assign a background color (or image) to all pages to which the style is linked (**Figure 10d**). Click the Apply button to preview the result.

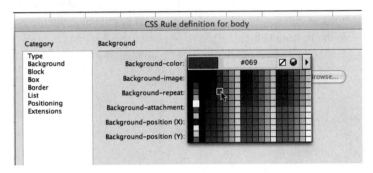

Figure 10d Defining a page background color.

7. Page margins are controlled by the Body tag. By default, Web pages display with a 10-pixel top and left margin, but this can be changed, and should be changed if you are using the 960 pixel-width page layout standards. In the Box category of the "CSS Rule Definition for body" dialog, enter **0** (zero) in the Top Margin box, and leave the Same for All check box selected.

(continued on next page)

Attaching an Existing CSS File to a Page

Once you create a CSS file, you can attach it to any open page using the Link icon at the bottom of the CSS Styles panel.

Create a CSS File Just Once

After creating a new external CSS file, you add more styles to the CSS file *without* creating a new style sheet. So, once you have created your first style and generated a CSS file, the *next* time you create a new style, click the New CSS Rule icon in the CSS Styles panel, but this time simply accept your existing CSS file in the New CSS Rule dialog.

8. After you create a style sheet file, the file is visible in the CSS Styles panel. When you expand the CSS file (click the triangle next to it to toggle to expand), all styles within the style will display. Formatting attributes display at the bottom of the CSS Styles panel (**Figure 10e**). You can edit styles in the CSS Styles panel by changing the attributes in the bottom half of the panel, or you can double-click on a style in the top half of the CSS Styles panel to edit it in the CSS Rule Definition dialog.

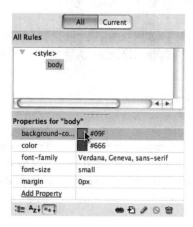

Figure 10e Viewing attributes for the Body tag in the CSS Styles panel.

#11 Creating Page Layouts with ID Styles

The essential building blocks of page design are div tags. These are HTML tags with no inherent properties—you get to assign any attributes you want to them, including size, location, background color, and float (alignment).

The div tag styles come in two basic flavors: ID and Class. ID div styles (ID styles for short) appear just once on a page, while Class div styles (Class styles for short) can be used over and over on a page. ID styles work well for defining page-layout elements, such as a container that will hold *all* the page content. In the following steps, I'll walk you through creating a single div tag to do just that.

To create an ID container and center it, follow these steps:

1. Open a document or create a new one. Attach an existing style sheet (see #10, "Creating and Linking a Style Sheet" earlier in this chapter).

2. In the CSS Styles panel, click the New CSS Rule icon. The New CSS Rule dialog opens.

3. In the Selector Type area of the dialog, choose ID. In the Selector Name area, enter a name with no spaces or special characters—if you want to follow my recipe here, call the style **container**.

(continued on next page)

div Tags vs. AP divs

Dreamweaver's Insert > Layout Objects menu has an option for AP divs. AP stands for absolute placement, and this menu option allows you to draw what are essentially ID div tags using familiar tools, and Dreamweaver generates CSS code to match. A somewhat less intuitive method of generating page layout with CSS in Dreamweaver CS4 is to define div tags. Although this feature has the advantage of being slightly more intuitive than defining ID divs "by hand" using the CSS Styles panel, the AP divs that are generated cannot be easily saved to an external style sheet. For that reason, we'll explore absolute placement ID div tags through a slightly different but better practice technique later in this chapter, in #14, "Using Absolute Placement."

div Overflow Options

The Visible option displays all content, even if it doesn't fit in the div. The Hidden option hides all content that does not fit in the div. The Scroll option displays a scrollbar, so the div looks like a miniature browser window with its own scrollbar(s). The Auto option leaves div display up to the user's browsing environment, so leave the Overflow display at Auto.

4. Choose your linked style sheet from the Choose Where Your Rule Will Be Defined pop-up menu **(Figure 11a).**

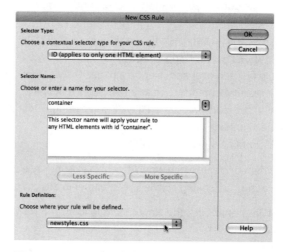

Figure 11a Preparing to define a new ID div tag.

5. Click OK in the New CSS Rule dialog. The CSS Rule Definition dialog for the style you are defining opens.

6. In the Background category, you can assign a background color (or image).

7. In the Box category in the CSS Rule Definition dialog, enter a width and height for the container—to create a 960-pixel-wide container, enter **960 px** in the Width boxes. Enter a height value as well. To center the div on a page, enter **Auto** for all margins.

8. There are a couple of options in the Positioning category relevant to defining a basic div container for a page. Visibility defines whether the div is visible. Unless you are designing div tags for a JavaScript application, leave the default setting at Visible. The Overflow pop-up menu defines how text that does not fit in the positioning object will appear in a browser.

9. Once you have defined the options in the Positioning category, you have defined the basic location and size of your div container. Use the Border category to apply borders to your object. Use the Box category to define buffer spacing between content and the box (Padding) or spacing between objects (Margin). Spacing is usually unnecessary with divs, but allowing 6 pixels of padding is often a good way to keep the content of different divs from bumping into each other.

10. When you have finished defining options for your div, click OK.

With your div defined, insert it on a page by choosing Insert > Layout Objects > Div Tag and selecting your div from the ID pop-up menu (**Figure 11b**).

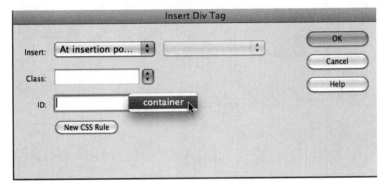

Figure 11b Inserting a div.

Enter content in your positioned div by clicking inside it and typing or by inserting images (**Figure 11c**). Or move on and work through #12, "Designing a Three-Column Layout," to increase the complexity of your page layout.

Figure 11c Inserting content into a positioned div.

Designing Web Pages in Dreamweaver with CSS Styles

#12 Designing a Three-Column Layout

In this How-To, I'll provide a recipe for implementing one of the most frequently used page layouts: a layout with three columns; two sidebars that are 25 percent of the width of the container; a center column that is 50 percent of the width of the container; a header; and a footer. Check the sidebar for instructions on how this can be adapted to other common layouts, like a 1/3, 1/3, 1/3 column layout.

To create the first layout, follow these steps:

1. Create the 960 container style in the previous How-To. That set of steps led you to create an external style sheet with a style called container.

2. Create a new page: select File > New, and from the Blank page category in the New Document dialog, choose HTML in the Page Type column and <none> in the Layout column. Save the page. If you're sticking with my recipe, call the page **960_model.html**. To reinforce the habit of assigning titles to all pages, even practice ones, enter a title in the Title box in the toolbar (something like **960 Grid Model**).

3. In the CSS Styles panel, click the Attach Style Sheet icon. The Attach External Style Sheet dialog opens. Navigate to and select the newstyles.css style sheet you created in the previous How-To. Or use another style sheet that has a 960-pixel-wide container style like the one defined in the previous How-To (**Figure 12a**).

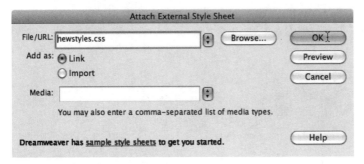

Figure 12a Attaching a style sheet.

(continued on next page)

4. With your cursor at the top of your new blank page, choose Insert > Layout Objects > Div Tag. From the Insert Div Tag dialog, choose Container from the ID pop-up menu. Or select another style if your 960-pixel-wide container has another style name (**Figure 12b**). A 960-pixel-wide ID style container appears on your page. This container will constrain the additional ID styles that will be used to create the header, footer, and three columns on your page.

Figure 12b Applying a 960-pixel-wide container style on a page.

5. Next, we'll place a style for the page header. Click and drag to select the text "Content for id 'container' Goes Here." You will replace this text with a new style for the header. Choose Insert > Layout Object > Div Tag. The Insert Div Tag dialog appears. Leave the Insert field set to Wrap Around Selection. In the ID field, type **header** (**Figure 12c**). Do *not* click OK. You still have to define the style. Click the New CSS Rule to open the New CSS Rule dialog.

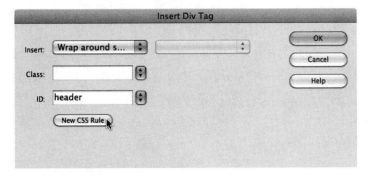

Figure 12c Creating a new layout style.

6. The New CSS Rule dialog is already filled out correctly based on what you entered in the Insert Div Tag dialog. Just click OK in this dialog (now you *can* click OK) to open the CSS Rule Definition dialog.

(continued on next page)

7. In the Background category, you can select a background color (or tiling image) if you wish. In the Box category, enter **100%** in the Width field and **100 pixels** in the Height box, and then choose Left from the Float pop-up menu (**Figure 12d**). Click OK to generate the style.

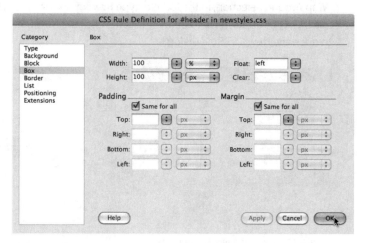

Figure 12d Defining a header style.

8. Next, we'll create a left-column style that takes 25 percent of the container width. There's a bit of a tricky step involved here. Remember, we are compiling CSS coding, and it's important that the coding for the column *not* be embedded in (inside of) the header you just created. You might want to jump to #16, "Using CSS Layout Pages," at this point for tips on understanding where you are generating code. Here's how to place the code properly: Hover over an edge of the header until your cursor becomes an arrow, and click to select the header. Then, use your right-arrow key on your keyboard to move just past this coding (**Figure 12e**).

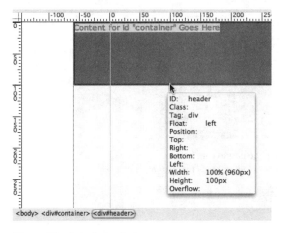

Figure 12e Selecting a div tag.

9. Choose Insert > Layout Object > Div Tag. The Insert Div Tag dialog appears. Enter **left_col** in the ID box and click the New CSS Rule button to open the New CSS Rule dialog. Click OK in this dialog and open the CSS Rule Definition dialog. In the Background Category, you can select a background color (or tiling image) if you wish. In the Box category, enter **25%** in the Width field and **600 pixels** in the Height box, and then choose Left from the Float pop-up menu. Click OK to generate the style. Click OK again to insert it on the page.

(continued on next page)

Headers and Footers

Headers are typically used to present a banner, navigational elements, a search box, a sign-up form, and other content. Footers are typically used to provide supplemental links, legal notices, and other secondary content.

Changing 25-50-25 to 1/3, 1/3, 1/3

The recipe in this How-To generates a three-column page with 2 one-quarter-page sidebars. You can change that to three columns of even width by entering a value of **33.3%** for each of the three columns.

Flexible Settings

You can adjust the recipe on this page to create your own page design by changing the values of the widths and heights of any of the div styles. Just remember, width has to *total* 100% for the columns; if you exceed that, your page layout will collapse as the columns won't fit in the main container.

10. Generate the next column (call it **center_col**) the same way, but enter **50%** in the Width field. Then, generate a third column (call it **right_col**), again the same way but enter **25%** in the Width field. Finally, generate the footer the same way you created the header in steps 5–7 (name this style **footer**). The trick is to pay attention to *where* your cursor is when you generate the CSS code and insert divs—for the footer, the cursor should be *inside* the main container div (**Figure 12f**).

Figure 12f A page design with header, footer, and three columns, ready for content.

#13 Designing with Class Styles

Class tags are more flexible than ID styles in that they can be reused multiple times on a page. In the next chapter, we'll explore how to use them to create font attributes, like highlighting, italics, or special type styles. Here, we'll create a box that can be placed anywhere on a page, with type flowing either to the left or the right of the box.

We will continue to work with and expand on the CSS file you created in #10, "Creating and Linking a Style Sheet." You can work with an existing page to which all the div tag styles created in this chapter have been applied, or with a blank page. But in either case, make sure you've linked your page to an external style sheet (or you can create a new one).

To create a Class style, click the New CSS Rule icon at the bottom of the CSS Styles panel. In the New CSS Rule dialog, choose Class from the Selector Type pop-up menu. In the Selector Name field, enter a name (avoid spaces or special characters). In the Rule Definition pop-up menu, choose your linked style sheet. Click OK in the New CSS Rule dialog to open the CSS Rule Definition dialog for your Class style.

The two categories you'll use to define a Class style for layout are Background (where you assign a background color or image) and Box, where you define the size of the layout box. Use Right float to flow type to the left of the box and Left float to flow type to the right of the box.

Perfect for Pictures

A Class style, like the one used twice Figure 13a, works well for displaying images in Web sites. You can create an appropriately sized class style and place an image inside, and then align the image by floating the class right or left. The Class style box can include a text caption as well.

Once created, you can insert a Class style box anywhere by choosing Insert > Layout Object > Div Tag and selecting a Class style from the Class pop-up menu in the Insert Div Tag dialog. **Figure 13a** shows a 120-pixel-square Class style with a yellow background and Float defined as Right. The style box has been inserted twice.

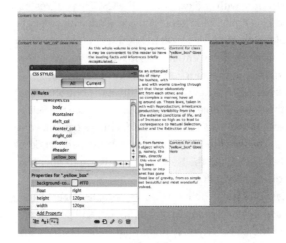

Figure 13a A Class style used twice on a page.

#14 Using Absolute Placement

Up to this point in this chapter, we've created page-layout styles (ID and Class styles associated with div tags) that are placed on a page at the insertion point. That is, they appear wherever they are inserted on a page. An alternate way of designing pages is to create div tags with absolute placement styles. Those styles appear at an exact point on a page—like 10 pixels from the top of the page, and 10 pixels from the left edge.

There are both design and accessibility implications for using absolute placement for div tags. They are easier to design, in Dreamweaver CS5 at least, because you can draw them, as you'll see shortly. They are less flexible than relatively placed divs. You cannot, for example, make one "25 percent" of the width of a page or container; they are of fixed widths.

To create an absolutely positioned div tag style, choose Insert > Layout Object > Div Tag. Because each absolutely positioned div will have a unique position, you will generally want to make them ID divs, not Class divs. Enter a name for the div in the ID field of the Insert Div Tag dialog, and click New CSS Rule (*not* OK). Click OK in the New CSS Rule dialog to jump to the CSS Rule Definition dialog.

You can define a background color for the div in the Background category of the CSS Rule Definition dialog. In the Positioning category, enter any values in the Width and Height fields (100 px works fine), and choose Absolute from the Position pop-up menu. Then click OK in the CSS Rule Definition dialog.

Are Absolutely Placed divs AP divs?

As I noted in a sidebar in #11, "Creating Page Layouts with ID Styles," the technique I'm introducing you to for creating absolutely positioned div tags has the advantages of Dreamweaver's somewhat proprietary "AP div" technique, while being more standard, and allowing you to save absolutely positioned divs to an external style sheet—something not readily available for Dreamweaver's AP divs. That said, the techniques in this How-To are similar to using the Insert > Layout Objects > AP Div option.

Caution: Avoid Mixing Absolute and Relative divs

It's generally a bad idea to mix absolute and relatively positioned div tags on a page because relatively sized divs (ones that are positioned at an insertion point, and/or have size defined as a percent) will tend to move on a page depending on changes in layout and viewing environment, while absolutely positioned divs always stay in the same place. Also, Absolute positioned divs don't work in a centered container as in the #container we created earlier.

The div that appears can be moved and resized directly in the Design window, interactively, without recourse to the CSS Styles panel. When you click to select the box, sizing handles appear on the corners and sides. Use them to resize the div. Use the grabber handle in the upper-left corner of a selected absolutely positioned div to move it (**Figure 14a**).

Figure 14a Moving an absolutely positioned div.

#15 Identifying and Editing CSS Elements

Dreamweaver CS5 allows you to apply identifying color backgrounds to CSS design boxes. These colors *do not* appear in a browser, but they help you sort through a page full of CSS div tags and figure out what's what so you can edit your page layout more easily.

To apply generated colors to CSS boxes, choose View > Visual Aids > CSS Layout Backgrounds. With CSS Styles Backgrounds turned on, CSS styles used as content containers display with distinct background colors (**Figure 15a**).

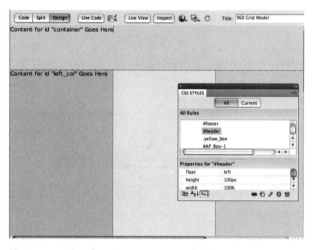

Figure 15a Identifying CSS containers with colors.

Assigning backgrounds to CSS boxes makes it easier to select those CSS styles, and view (or edit) their attributes in the CSS Styles panel. With a CSS container identified, you can easily edit style rules (attributes)—like box width, background color, padding, and so on—in the bottom of the CSS Styles panel, or by double-clicking on the applicable CSS Rule in the top of the panel to open the Rule Definition dialog. Either technique works.

To turn off layout background colors and view actual background colors on your page, choose View > Visual Aids, and deselect CSS Layout Backgrounds.

Editing CSS in the CSS Styles Panel

You can access all the attributes of a CSS style by double-clicking on it in the CSS Styles panel and opening it in the CSS Rule Definition dialog. But a simpler way is to make quick, interactive adjustments to the parameters of a CSS div tag used as a positioning box. When you select the tag in the CSS Styles panel, the defined parameters for the selected CSS style display in a handy table at the bottom of the CSS Styles panel. Each parameter is editable within the CSS Styles panel: Just enter or select a new value for any displayed parameter.

#16 Using CSS Layout Pages

Dreamweaver CS5 includes an updated and revamped set of CSS-based layout pages. To create a new page using these layouts, choose File > New, select the Blank Page category, and choose HTML in the Page Type list.

If you've worked through this chapter, you'll recognize that these CSS page layouts are built on the same kinds of defined div tags explored in the previous How-Tos.

You can preview the available CSS page layouts, like "3 column fixed, header and footer" selected in **Figure 16a**, by clicking on them once.

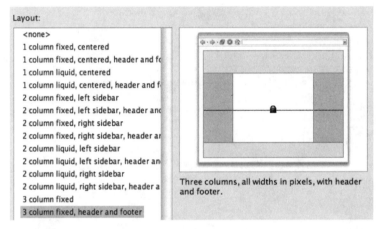

Layout:

```
<none>
1 column fixed, centered
1 column fixed, centered, header and f
1 column liquid, centered
1 column liquid, centered, header and f
2 column fixed, left sidebar
2 column fixed, left sidebar, header and
2 column fixed, right sidebar
2 column fixed, right sidebar, header a
2 column liquid, left sidebar
2 column liquid, left sidebar, header an
2 column liquid, right sidebar
2 column liquid, right sidebar, header a
3 column fixed
3 column fixed, header and footer
```

Three columns, all widths in pixels, with header and footer.

Figure 16a Previewing a CSS layout.

The CSS Layouts available in the New Document dialog are well docu-mented. There's no need to study the coding; you just study the provided dummy text, which explains how the style works.

Standards Applied to CSS Layouts

The CSS layouts in Dreamweaver CS5 are remarkably standards-compliant. The layouts are 960 pixels wide. They are supported in all modern browsers, including Internet Explorer 6, which tends to not support a number of CSS attributes that work in other browsers. They include template logos that you replace, of course.

CHAPTER THREE

Formatting Text and Embedding Images

Assigning type formatting for Web pages, compared to print typography, has two significant limitations:

- On the Web, you cannot control what fonts are installed on a viewer's browser.

- On the Web, screen resolution (72 pixels per inch) is much lower than in print, where even a low-cost home printer can produce four times the resolution available on a viewing device.

These limitations mean that you cannot just pick any font you have on your computer, assign it to text, and expect that it will appear in a visitor's monitor. Instead, Web fonts are generally widely used standards, and are grouped with "backup" fonts that display if a viewer does not have the first-choice font installed.

Within those limits, you can format type on the Web in much the same way you would in print. As CSS has evolved, so too has the ability to format type. In this chapter, I'll show you how to apply fonts, font sizes, font colors, line and word spacing, and other type attributes, as well as style attributes for links, graphics, and printable pages.

In this chapter, you'll also learn to embed images and use Dreamweaver's limited set of image-editing tools.

Finally, I'll show you how to apply type styling to Web sites created with content management systems (CMSs) like Drupal, WordPress, and Joomla! (I'll use Drupal as an example, but the process is similar.) These CMS programs generate content but have limited and clunky tools for formatting type. Dreamweaver CS5 includes radical new features that allow you to access and edit that formatting.

Throughout this chapter, consistent with the approach of this entire book toward Web design with Adobe CS5, our model will be a Web site with an external style sheet. Before diving into the style techniques in this chapter, you will find it helpful to review Chapter 2, "Designing Web Pages in Dreamweaver with CSS Styles."

#17 Defining Font Tag Styles

Body Is the Default, but Other Tag Formatting Overrides the Default

In #10, "Creating and Linking a Style Sheet," in Chapter 2, I showed you how to assign style attributes to the Body tag. The Body tag applies to both page-layout elements (like background color and margins) and type formatting. The type format you assign to the Body tag (like font family) becomes the default setting for all type tags in your style sheet. But when you define particular type tags (like p, for paragraph, or H1 for Heading 1), those particular settings override the formatting applied by the Body tag.

At the foundation of every Web page is HTML (Hypertext Markup Language). HTML assigns *tags* to everything on a page. CSS (Cascading Style Sheets) are then used to format those tags.

Here are the basic HTML text-formatting tags:

- Paragraph tag, which defines most paragraph text

- Headings 1–6, which define headings (Heading 1 is the largest)

- Unordered lists, which are bullet point lists, and ordered lists, which are numbered lists

The first and basic step in formatting type for a Web site is to create CSS rules for each of these tags, and save them to the external style sheet that controls the appearance of the Web site. In Chapter 2, we created a style sheet called newstyle.css. We'll continue to use that style sheet here, but you can create a different one if you choose. In either case, the following instructions assume you have created a new Web page, saved it, placed text on it, and linked that page to a CSS file (a style sheet).

To define the formatting of any text tag, click the New CSS Rule icon in the CSS Styles panel. In the New CSS Rule dialog, choose Tag as the Selector Type. From the Selector Name drop-down menu, choose a tag to define: P is Paragraph, and H1–H6 are the six header tags. In the Rule Definition drop-down menu, select the external style sheet you have linked to the open page. Then click OK to open the CSS Rule Definition dialog (**Figure 17a**).

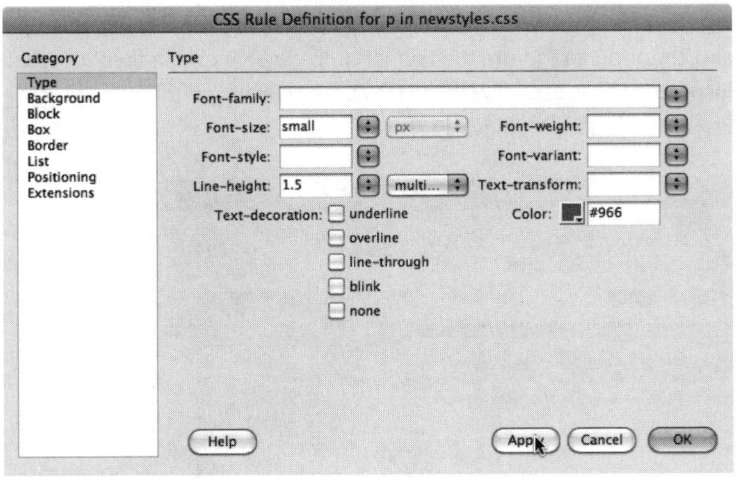

Figure 17a Defining the paragraph (p) tag.

In the Type category of the CSS Rule Definition dialog, use the Font-family drop-down menu to choose a group of fonts to assign to P (paragraph tag) text.

Use the Font-size drop-down menu to define font size, Font-weight to apply various shades of boldface, Font-style to apply (or turn off) italics, Font-variant to apply (or turn off) small caps, and Text-transform to change case.

Line-height defines the distance between lines. Use the Color swatch to assign a type color. The Text-decoration set of check boxes is most useful as a way to turn underlining off, or on, for various link states.

So Many Ways to Define Font Size

There are many—probably too many—ways to define font size in CSS. You can define absolute values and units of measurement (like 12 points, 10 pixels, or 1 em). You can use relative sizes (small, medium, large). And after all that, the actual size of type that viewers see will depend to a great extent on their viewing environment (type is noticeably larger, for example, on PCs than on Macs). The best solution depends a great deal on your audience. If I had to pick a one-size-fits-all recommendation, I'd suggest going with one of the relative measurements (larger if you prefer relatively large type, smaller for smaller, or nothing if you prefer standard Web-sized type).

Airing Out Pages with Line Height

Line height is an underrated way to make your type more inviting. Assigning a Line-height value of 1.5 multiple, for example, creates one-and-a-half line spacing. This is not as airy as double spacing between lines but still creates a lot of air on type-heavy pages.

Preview with Apply

Here's the most important thing to know about defining font tags: You can experiment with different attributes in the CSS Rule Definition dialog, and use the Apply button to preview how they will look on the page.

Most type formatting is done in the Type category of the CSS Rule Definition dialog. But you can assign background colors in the Background category, word and letter spacing in the Block category, and indenting in the Box category (enter values in the Padding fields to indent text left and/or right).

After you define attributes for a text tag, click OK in the CSS Rule Definition dialog.

Once you have defined attributes for the paragraph tag and heading tags, you assign those tags to text by clicking *anywhere in a paragraph* and choosing a tag from the Format drop-down menu in the Properties inspector. This is easiest with the HTML tab selected on the left side of the Properties inspector (**Figure 17b**).

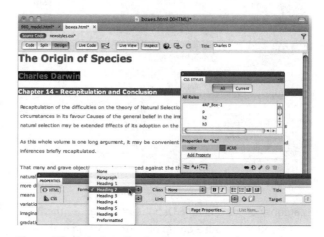

Figure 17b Assigning a Heading 2 tag to a selected paragraph.

#18 Text Formatting with Class Styles

Class styles for fonts are defined pretty much the same way tag styles are. But there is a difference: they are tag *independent*. So, for instance, if you create a Class style that applies red font color, italics, and yellow highlighting to text, you can apply that Class style to all or part of text in a Heading 1 paragraph, a p (paragraph) paragraph, or any other paragraph.

To create a new Class style, click the New CSS Rule icon in the CSS Styles panel. In the New CSS Rule dialog, choose Class as the Selector Type. In the Selector Name field, enter a name that describes the style (like **red_type_yellow_highlite**). Avoid spaces and special characters. Save Class styles, like all styles, in the external style sheet you are using for your site—do this in the Rule Definition section of the New CSS Rule dialog—and then click OK.

In the CSS Rule Definition dialog, define text attributes for the Class style you are creating (again, the process is the same as for defining CSS styles for text tags, which we explored in the previous How-To). Click OK to generate the Class style.

Apply Class styles by clicking and dragging to select text and then choosing a Class style from the Class drop-down menu in the Properties inspector (**Figure 18a**).

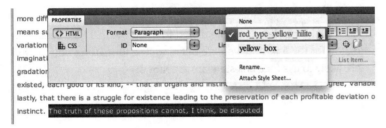

Figure 18a Applying a Class style to selected text within a paragraph.

Don't Overdo Class Styles

There is a tendency to create billions of Class styles for Web sites. It's better to try to rely on HTML tag styles (like paragraph, Heading 1, etc.) for most of your formatting. This ensures a uniform look and feel across your site. It makes it easier to change that look and feel (by reformatting HTML tag styles). And it keeps your style sheet as uncluttered as possible.

#**19** Formatting Links

By default, links are displayed in blue type (or blue borders for images). Visited links are purple, and active links (ones in the process of being opened) are red. By default, all links display with underlining. You can customize the appearance and behavior of links using CSS. CSS formatting is applied to links so widely that people tend to expect to find features like rollover display or nonunderlined links on sites.

CSS formatting allows you to define four link states. In addition to the three HTML states (regular, visited, and active links), CSS can define a fourth state—hover. Hover state displays when a visitor hovers the mouse cursor over the link. Dreamweaver CS5 allows you to preview all link states (plus "focus" state—see sidebar).

To create a CSS formatting *rule* (style), follow these steps:

1. With a page open, click the New CSS Rule icon in the CSS Styles panel. The New CSS Rule dialog opens.

2. From the Selector Type pop-up menu, choose Compound. From the Selector Name pop-up menu, choose one of the four link states: link, visited, hover, or active.

3. In the Rule Definition area of the dialog, select the style sheet linked to your site.

4. Click OK in the New CSS Rule dialog to open the CSS Rule Definition dialog for the link state you are defining. The formatting options you are likely to use for a link state are as follows:

About Focus State

Focus state is for those who navigate through a site using the tab key to go from link to link or form field to form field. It lets them see where they are.

Style Approaches Used for Hover Link Formatting

Sometimes, designers turn off underlining for all other link states but will have it appear when a visitor hovers over a link. Other times, designers define a color or background-display change when a link is hovered over.

Never Assign Font or Font Size to Links!

Normally, you will *not* define font or font size to link style definitions. That's because links inherit the font and font size of the HTML formatting tag assigned to the text. For example, Heading 1 (h1) text might include text that is a link.

(continued on next page)

Formatting Text and Embedding Images

- **Type category:** Allows you to define a color for the selected link state using the Color box. The check boxes in the Text-decoration area allow you to turn underlining on or off. By default, links are underlined, so select the None check box to turn *off* underlining. Simply deselecting the Underline check box will not turn off underlining (**Figure 19a**).

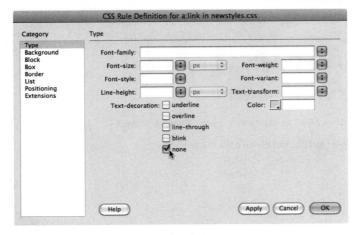

Figure 19a Turning off underlining for a link state.

- **Background category:** Allows you to define a background color or image behind the selected text.

5. After you define a CSS link style, click OK to automatically apply it to an external style sheet or to your page (depending on the selection you made in the Define in section of the New CSS Rule dialog when you began defining the style).

Or paragraph text might include some text that functions as a link. In either case, the font and font size will not change for the link text.

What often *will* change is font color and maybe font attributes like underlining or background. So, when you define CSS styles for links, you will normally avoid defining font or font size and instead define font color and special attributes (like underlining or background).

Defining Four Link States

You will define each of the four link states separately. Link (unvisited link), visited, hover, and active are each a unique style. For these link styles to be interpreted correctly in browsers, you need to create them in just that order. If you need to reorder styles, you can click on any style in the CSS Styles panel and drag it up or down in the panel to reorder.

With Dreamweaver CS5's new Rendering tools, you can see the effect of any link in Design view even with Live View turned off. Display Rendering tools by choosing View > Toolbars > Style Rendering if that toolbar is not displayed. Then choose a link state to preview (**Figure 19b**).

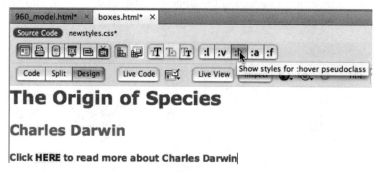

Figure 19b Previewing a link in hovered state.

Formatting Text and Embedding Images

#20 Embedding Images

There are essentially two ways to embed images in Web pages with Dreamweaver CS5. One is to prepare the artwork in Photoshop, Illustrator, Fireworks, or other image-editing or drawing programs, and export it for the Web using CS5's Save for Web & Devices window. That's preferable. The second is to copy and paste artwork directly into Dreamweaver. That's less robust but works in a pinch, for prototyping or when you're just in a hurry. We'll explore both options here.

To embed (place on a Web page) an image that has already been sized and prepared for the Web in Photoshop, Illustrator, or another image-editing or drawing tool, place your cursor at the insertion point where the image should appear and choose Insert > Image. The Select Image Source dialog appears. Navigate to the image, and click Choose to insert the image. You'll be prompted for Alternate text—enter that and click OK to place the image in your Web page.

If you copy and paste an image into Dreamweaver, or use the steps in the previous paragraph to insert an image in Photoshop (PSD) format, the Image Preview dialog opens. This is Dreamweaver's utility for converting images to Web-compatible formats (JPEG, GIF, or PNG). As the Save for Web & Devices tools in Illustrator and Photoshop are much more robust, we'll explore options for preparing images for the Web in those chapters of this book, and just take a quick look at Dreamweaver's Image Preview. On the Options tab, you can choose an image format from the Format drop-down menu, image quality from the Quality slider, smoothing (blurring), and a few other options.

Preparing Images for the Web

For instructions on how to prepare images for the Web, see Chapter 8, "Preparing Photos for the Web with Photoshop," and Chapter 10, "Creating Artwork for the Web in Illustrator."

Applying a Style Sheet to Images

Any HTML tag can have a CSS style associated with it, and that applies to the IMG tag that is used to embed images. You might, for example, want to associate horizontal and vertical spacing with every image, to keep them from bumping up against text or each other. Doing this as a CSS style ensures that images will have uniform spacing throughout your site, and it won't be necessary to assign image spacing to every image as you embed it on a page.

Insert Image and Formats

Using the Insert > Image command works only with Web-compliant formats (JPEG, PNG, and GIF) and PSD files. You must use copy/paste with other formats.

Progressive and Transparency Options

The Progressive option (for JPEG and PNG) should usually be selected—it allows images to "fade in" when there is a slow Internet connection, rather than appear line by line. PNG and GIF images can have a transparent color selected—that color disappears and the Web-page background shows through instead.

There is a 4-up option on the Options tab of the Image Preview window that allows you to experiment with different formats, settings, and options (**Figure 20a**).

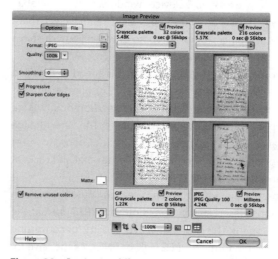

Figure 20a Previewing different import options for an image copied into Dreamweaver.

The File tab of the Image Preview window allows you to resize images. By selecting the Constrain check box, you maintain the original height-to-width ratio as you resize.

Click OK to embed your image after you define settings in the Image Preview window.

There are two properties you will likely want to assign to embedded images in the Properties inspector. Using the H space and V space boxes creates a buffer space around the image—I generally use 2 pixels vertical spacing and 5 pixels horizontal spacing. Choosing either Left or Right Align from the Align drop-down menu flows text around your image (**Figure 20b**).

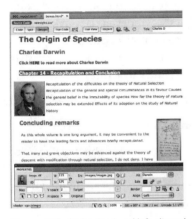

Figure 20b Right- (top) and left-aligned (bottom) images with horizontal and vertical spacing.

Alt Tag and Accessibility

By default, when you insert an image, the Image Tag Accessibility Attributes dialog opens and prompts you for Alternate text. This text is used by people with sight disabilities or those whose browsing environment does not support images, and displays if the image is corrupted. Enter a short description of the image. The Long Description prompt in the dialog allows you to link to an HTML text file that consists of a long description of the image. That level of accessibility is not always necessary, but it's helpful if your audience includes a large number of people who cannot access images.

#21 Creating CSS for Printable Pages

Creating a Style Sheet?

Review the techniques discussed in Chapter 2, "Designing Web Pages in Dreamweaver with CSS Styles," for all the information you need to create an external style sheet.

Many times you will want to define different styles for printed pages than you use for monitor display. For example, you might change a light-colored font to black for printing or remove page or table background images. You do this by creating and attaching a separate CSS file—a separate external style sheet—that holds print-formatting rules. You can also preview in the Document window how a page will look when printed.

To define a new style sheet for printer output, you can create an external style sheet with CSS tag styles, link styles, or even class styles. Name the external style sheet that contains the print styles **print.css**.

After you define a distinct set of printable styles in the print.css style sheet file, attach the print.css file as the printer style sheet:

1. Open the Web page to which the printer CSS styles will be attached.

2. In the CSS Styles panel, click the Attach Style Sheet (link) icon.

3. In the File/URL field of the Attach External Style Sheet dialog, click Browse and navigate to the print.css file. Click OK (Windows) or Choose (Mac). The Attach External Style Sheet dialog appears. In the Add as area, leave the Link radio button selected.

4. From the Media pop-up menu, choose print (**Figure 21a**).

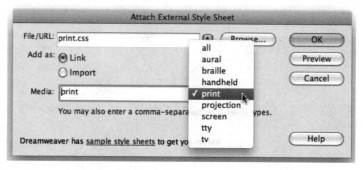

Figure 21a Defining print.css as the printer style sheet.

To preview your printer styles, click the Render Print Media Type icon in the Style Rendering toolbar (**Figure 21b**). If the Style Rendering toolbar is not visible, choose View > Toolbars > Style Rendering.

Figure 21b Clicking the Render Print Media Type icon in the Style Rendering toolbar.

One class style attribute that is only relevant to print style sheets is the page-break attribute. To define a page break in the printed version of a Web page, follow these steps:

1. Click the New CSS Rule icon in the CSS Styles panel. The New CSS Rule dialog opens.

2. In the Selector Type area of the dialog, choose Class (can apply to any tag) from the pop-up menu. From the Selector Name pop-up menu, choose a style name, such as page_break.

3. In the Rule Definition area of the dialog, choose your print.css external style sheet from the pop-up menu. Click OK in the New CSS Rule dialog to open the CSS Rule Definition dialog.

4. In the CSS Rule Definition dialog, choose the Extensions category. In the Page-Break-After field, choose Always from the pop-up menu.

After you define a page-break style, you can apply it anywhere by inserting the style from the Properties inspector.

More than One CSS File Per Page?

Yes. You can attach multiple style sheets to a page and define different CSS files to different media using the same process.

Useful Print Formatting

Useful special formatting features for printed versions of pages include the following:

- **No colored print:** Some people print documents on laser printers that print only in black.

- **No backgrounds:** They interfere with readability.

- **Different margins:** They accommodate standard 8.5-inch-wide paper.

- **Page breaks:** They break content into discrete sections.

#22 Connecting Dreamweaver to a CMS Site

FTP Tips for Connecting Dreamweaver to a CMS Site

When you define the remote connection to a CMS site as part of a Dreamweaver site definition, select the Live and Staging check boxes next to the server connection you just defined. You'll need those features enabled to detect and edit CMS formatting in Dreamweaver CS5. One other tip for making an FTP connection in Dreamweaver to a CMS site: The CMS site is likely to reside in a root directory (like public_html) on the server.

Don't Edit CMS *Content* in Dreamweaver CS5

You are not going to edit your CMS page content in Dreamweaver. Page content in CMS programs is generated in an entirely different way than creating pages in Dreamweaver.

(continued on next page)

Perhaps the most dramatic addition to Dreamweaver CS5 is the ability to mesh with CMS sites created using applications like Drupal, Joomla!, or WordPress. These programs make powerful database tools widely accessible. Dreamweaver can detect database connections in CMS pages, but editing those in Dreamweaver is beyond the scope of this book, and most people will rely on database tools in the CMS to manage those connections. Of wider interest and more value is the ability of Dreamweaver CS5 to detect CSS styles associated with pages in CMS sites and edit that CMS.

That process has two steps. The first is to connect Dreamweaver to your CMS site, and the second is to detect and edit the CSS in the CMS site. In this How-To, I'll focus on the connection part. In the next How-To, I'll show you how to detect and edit CSS in a CMS.

To connect to a CMS site, you'll need the same basic FTP login information you would need when you set up any Dreamweaver remote site. Refer back to Chapter 1, "Creating a Web Site in Dreamweaver CS5," for a complete exploration of that process.

With a local and remote site defined (again, use the connection settings provided by your Web host, not the CMS administrator), follow these steps to connect your CMS site to Dreamweaver, and open your CMS home page in Dreamweaver CS5:

1. Choose Window > Files to open the Files panel in Dreamweaver CS5. Click the Expand icon in the Files panel toolbar to view both the local and remote versions of your CMS site.

2. Click the Connects to Local Host icon in the expanded Files panel toolbar to connect to the remote site.

3. It is not necessary to download the entire CMS site. Instead, navigate to the file index.php in the root folder of the CMS site. This is the file that displays content on the home page of the site. Double-click on that file to open it in Dreamweaver. At the Get Dependent Files prompt, select Yes.

4. Click the Discover link at the top of the page in Dreamweaver page view.

5. Note the Script Warning dialog if it is enabled—it's telling you that you are essentially opening all the files in Dreamweaver that are used to produce the CMS Web page. That's just what you want to do, so select Yes.

6. A list of files will appear in the External Files tabs at the top of the Design window. Many of these files are related to the database that supplies content to the page. Others, with .css filename extensions, are style sheets that control the appearance of sections of this, and other, pages. It is those files that you will detect and edit. You can filter for just CSS files by using the Filter for Related Files icon in the External Files tabs (see **Figure 22a**).

7. To see the content that is packaged into the CMS home page, you need to view the page in Live view. Click the Live View button or the Live View link at the top of the page to display the content that appears in the Drupal home page. Again, select Yes if any warning dialogs appear.

Figure 22a Viewing a Drupal site and related CSS files in Live view in Dreamweaver CS5.

With your CMS site now synched with Dreamweaver, you're ready to edit the CSS on that site.

Users enter content into forms in their CMS application, and that content automatically gets plugged into the site in a manner defined by the site administrator. You *will* be opening pages from your CMS site in Dreamweaver's Design view, but only as a means to an end: identifying and editing the CSS styles that are applied to the entire site.

No Content on CMS Home Page?

When you first connect to your CMS home page through Dreamweaver CS5, the CMS home page won't be much to look at. It's actually just a container that holds content supplied by a database at the site. But Dreamweaver will help connect all the necessary files so you can see what the page looks like.

#23 Formatting CMS Themes

Once you open your CMS home page in Dreamweaver's Live view (see #22, "Connecting Dreamweaver to a CMS Site,"), you can use the CSS panel in Dreamweaver to change your CMS Theme and apply all the CSS styles techniques covered in this and the previous chapter to a CMS site.

To edit the CSS in your CMS site, display the CSS Styles panel (Window > CSS Styles). On the All tab of the CSS Styles panel, you'll see several CSS files listed. These files control all the formatting in your CMS site.

Examine the styles. You will edit them just as you would edit styles in a normal Dreamweaver site (**Figure 23a**).

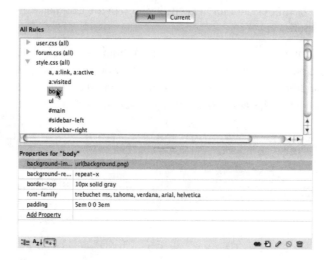

Figure 23a Examining CSS styles in a Drupal Web site.

As you begin to edit the CSS styles in your CMS site, Dreamweaver will prompt you to download those CSS files that are required. Click the Get link that appears to download those files. Dreamweaver may periodically prompt you to discover and download additional associated files to make changes to the CMS site.

As you edit CSS content (**Figure 23b**), an asterisk (*) appears in the External Files tab indicating CSS files that have been changed locally and that need to be saved and uploaded. After you make changes to those CSS files, select them in the External Files tab and use Dreamweaver's Put option to upload them back to the server.

Figure 23b Changing font color in the Body tag of a Drupal site in Dreamweaver CS5. Note that styles.css appears with an asterisk in the External Files tab indicating it has been changed and must be saved and uploaded.

Uploading a Changed CSS File

1. Control-click (Mac) or right-click (Windows) on the styles.css* file (or other changed CSS files) in the list of external files at the top of the Dreamweaver Design window. Choose Open As Separate File from the context menu (the * at the end of the file name means the file needs to be saved).

2. Choose File > Save to save changes to the style sheet that you made while editing styles in the index.php page.

3. In the Document toolbar (choose View > Toolbars > Document if it is not visible), select Put. This uploads the file to the CMS site server.

4. Open your CMS site in a browser, and refresh/reload the view. The changes you defined in Dreamweaver will be applied sitewide.

CHAPTER FOUR

Collecting Data in Forms

Forms provide a uniquely interactive element in a Web site. Through a form you not only *convey* content, you also *collect* content. This content can range from orders for products, feedback on site content, service requests, and subscription list sign-ups to surveys, forum discussions, and opinion polls.

Some form content is managed using scripts that run in the visitor's browser. Such scripts are referred to as *client-side* data handling. A jump menu, for example, collects data (the page a visitor to your Web site wants to go to, for example) and acts on that input (by opening a new Web page). The client-side script does that *without* sending any data to a server. Other forms collect data and send it to a server, where scripts on the server manage the data. These are called *server-side* forms. Most form data is managed by server-side scripts. One example of a server-side script is a mailing list form. Visitors enter information (at least an email address and maybe more) into a form. That data is then stored in a database on a remote server. It can be accessed to send out mailings.

In short, this chapter explains how to design two kinds of forms:

- Forms that manage data in the browser (client-side)

- Forms that connect to scripts at a server (server-side)

In this chapter, you'll learn how to connect a form to an existing server script (but not how to program the scripts). I've also thrown in some tips on where you can find already-packaged server scripts to handle things like search forms, sign-up mailing lists, and discussion forums.

#24 Creating Jump Menus

One great example of a client-side form is a jump menu from which a visitor selects a page in your Web site from a pop-up menu. A jump menu works because script (in this case, JavaScript) acts on a form and effects an action (in this case, opening a new Web page) based on data the visitor entered into the form (the page the visitor chose from the jump menu). Dreamweaver creates jump menu forms and automatically generates the required JavaScript.

Jump menus are an efficient and attractive way to allow visitors to navigate your site. You can provide a long list of target links in a jump menu without using much valuable space on your Web page.

To create a jump menu, follow these steps:

1. With a page open in the Document window, choose Insert > Form > Jump Menu. The Insert Jump Menu dialog opens.

2. Use the Text field to name each menu item—enter text that will appear in the jump menu.

   Note
   The text you enter in the Text field defines the name of the menu item. You don't have to enter anything in the Menu Item field; that information is automatically generated by what you type in the Text field.

3. In the "When selected, go to URL" field, either enter a URL for a link or use the Browse button to navigate to and select a file on your site.

4. Define additional jump menu options by clicking the plus button in the dialog and entering new text and URLs. Repeat to enter as many jump menu options as you need. Delete an item from the jump menu by selecting it and clicking the minus button.

5. To change the order of an item in the jump menu list, select the item and use the Up and Down arrow buttons in the dialog to move the selected item up or down in the list.

6. After you define all the links in the jump menu, click OK to generate the menu. Test the menu in a browser (you can't test it in the Dreamweaver Document window because the jump menu works with JavaScript in a browser).

To edit an existing jump menu, you need to open the behavior that Dreamweaver created to control the jump menu. View the Behaviors panel (choose Window > Behaviors). Click the jump menu to select it. As you do, you will see Jump Menu listed in the second column of the Behaviors panel. Double-click it to reopen the Jump Menu dialog and edit the jump menu (**Figure 24a**).

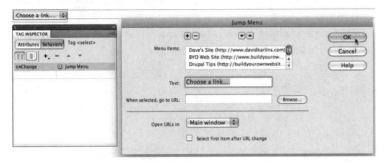

Figure 24a Opening the Jump Menu dialog by double-clicking Jump Menu in the Behaviors panel.

The Jump Menu dialog looks just like the Insert Jump Menu dialog, and you can add, remove, or move menu items or change menu options in this dialog.

Jump Menu Details

In the Insert Jump Menu dialog, the "Open URLs in" field allows you to define a frame in which to open a linked page. It applies only if you are working in frames. The Menu name field is automatically filled out by Dreamweaver and enables Dreamweaver to generate JavaScript to manage the input. In the Options area of the dialog, the "Insert go button after menu" check box generates a Go button for your jump menu. The Go button is not reliably supported by browsers and should be avoided. The "Select first item after URL change" check box automatically places the first jump menu option as the selected choice after the jump menu is used to navigate to a page.

#25 Generating Forms

Form data is collected using different kinds of form fields. Text is entered into text boxes or text areas. Options can be selected from sets of radio buttons. Data can be uploaded using file fields. Forms are submitted (or cleared) using Submit (or Reset) buttons.

To create a form in an open Web page in Dreamweaver, simply click to place the location of the form and choose Insert > Form > Form. The form displays as a dashed red box. The Properties inspector displays the form name.

Make sure you have clicked *inside the form* before you add any form fields (**Figure 25a**).

Figure 25a A form placed on a page in Dreamweaver.

To activate prompts for accessibility options in forms, choose Edit > Preferences (Windows) or Dreamweaver > Preferences (Mac) and select the Accessibility category. Select the Form objects check box if it is not already selected. With form accessibility options activated, Dreamweaver prompts you with the Input Tag Accessibility Attributes dialog when you insert a form field into a form. The accessibility options allow visitors to fill out the form without using a mouse, or if they are relying on reader software, to have an identifying label read to them.

Form *Fields* Only Work in *Forms*

It's important to be conscious of this. Many of my students get frustrated trying to figure out why their sets of form fields aren't doing anything when the problem is that those form fields are not nested inside a form. A page can have more than one form. That's often not a good idea from a design standpoint, but you can imagine situations in which you might give visitors a choice of different forms to fill out.

Accessible Forms

Forms can be a big challenge for visitors with disabilities. Form accessibility issues include making it easy for disabled visitors (who, for example, cannot use a mouse) to move from field to field in a form and to easily select form fields. Dreamweaver CS5 promotes accessibility in many ways, including form design. If you enable accessibility preferences for form design, Dreamweaver prompts you to enter accessibility features for each form field as you place it in the form.

#26 Inserting Form Fields

Form fields are used within a form to collect data. The main, most widely used field types are text boxes, drop-down menus, sets of radio (option) buttons, and check boxes.

Text fields are used to collect all kinds of information in a form. Email addresses, phone numbers, purchase prices, zip codes, names, and a wide variety of other data can be entered into text fields.

Text *fields* collect a single line of text. Text *areas* can collect multiple lines of text. Text areas are used to collect comments, descriptions (like descriptions of problems for online service forms), guestbook entries, and other text that requires more than one line.

To place a text field or a text area in a form, follow these steps:

1. With your cursor *inside an existing form*, choose Insert > Form > Text Field or Insert > Form > Text Area.

2. After you place the text field, you can define the field attributes in the Properties inspector (**Figure 26a**). In the TextField field, enter a name that will help you remember the content of the field. In the Char width field, enter the number of characters that will display on a single line in a browser as a visitor enters data.

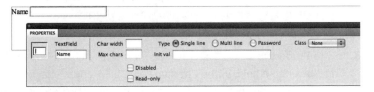

Figure 26a Defining a one-line text field.

3. In the Max chars field, you can enter the maximum number of characters that can be entered into the field.

4. In the Init val field, enter text that will appear in the field in a browser before any user interaction. Sometimes (but not always) form designers will include text like "your email goes here" in a field. Visitors then replace that content with their own entry.

5. In the Type options, choose Single line for a text field and Multiline for a text area. If you choose Multiline, the Num Lines field appears in the Properties inspector. Enter the number of lines that will display in the

(continued on next page)

How Many Characters Are Too Many for a Form Field?

Some thought needs to go into how many characters you elect to allow in a comment field. My friendly HMO, for instance, allows for something like 25 characters or fewer to describe my medical condition, providing a nice way to raise my frustration level when I need to communicate with the HMO and can't get through by phone! I can only hope other constraints are set more reasonably. There is a point to preventing someone from sending you his or her upcoming screenplay in a comment box.

What Are Image Fields?

Image fields are images in a form. They are sometimes used to create customized Submit or Reset buttons, but doing that takes scripting that is not directly available in Dreamweaver.

If you want to place an image field, choose Insert > Form > Image Field. When you do, the Select Image Source dialog opens, and you can navigate to and choose an image to insert into the form.

Using Fieldsets for Design

A fieldset is a design tool used to draw boxes around sections of a form. Fieldsets are particularly useful if you have a long form. Long forms tend to be intimidating or confusing, but by breaking groups of fields into boxed fieldsets, you can make your form more inviting and less overwhelming. You can also use fieldsets to emphasize a set of fields in a form. For example, if there is some information that is required or that you particularly want to collect, you can enclose that group of fields in a fieldset.

Placing a Fieldset

To place a fieldset in a form, first make sure your cursor is inside the form. You don't need to worry, initially, about the placement of the form fields you want to enclose in the fieldset. You can cut and paste them into the fieldset after you create it. Or you can click and drag to select the fields you want to include in the fieldset and then create the fieldset—that way, the fields are automatically

(continued on next page)

form (you cannot define a limit for the number of characters that are entered).

6. Enable the Password option only if you wish to display content entered into the field as asterisks.

7. You can use the Class pop-up menu to attach a CSS Class style to the field.

Tip

As you define text field or text area attributes in the Properties inspector, they display in the Document window.

You can place any number of check boxes in a form. Check boxes provide two options for visitors: Checked or Unchecked. You can define a default state for a check box as either checked or unchecked.

To place a check box in a form, follow these steps:

1. With your cursor inside an existing form, choose Insert > Form > Checkbox.

2. After you place the check box, if you did not generate a label, you need to enter some text in the form (normally to the right of the check box) that identifies what is being selected when a visitor selects the check box.

3. In the Properties inspector, enter a name for the check box in the Checkbox name field. In the Checked value field, enter a value to go with the check box name. For example, if the check box asks if a user wants to be contacted, the check box name might be "contact" and the checked value might be "yes."

4. Select one of the Initial state options to define whether the default state of the check box is Checked or Unchecked (**Figure 26b**).

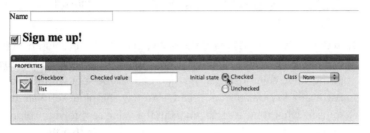

Figure 26b Defining a check box.

Radio buttons differ from check boxes in that they are always organized in groups. You never have a single radio button—if you are asking a question for which a user can supply no, one, or several answers, use check boxes. The purpose of radio buttons is to compel a user to choose *one* from a *group* of options.

To create a radio button group, follow these steps:

1. With your cursor inside an existing form, choose Insert > Form > Radio Group. The Radio Group dialog appears (**Figure 26c**).

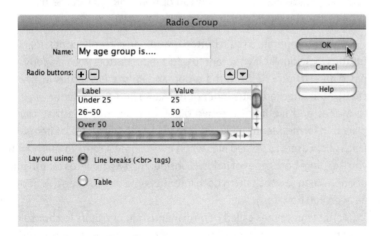

Figure 26c Defining a group of radio buttons.

(continued on next page)

enclosed in the fieldset. With your cursor inside a form, choose Insert > Form > Fieldset. The Fieldset dialog appears. In the Legend box, type a name that will appear at the top-left corner of the fieldset. This is the label that visitors will read when they see the form in their browsers.

Attaching Class Styles to Text Fields

You can use the Class pop-up menu in the Properties inspector to attach a CSS Class style to any field. However, this is sometimes especially handy for text (or text area) fields because you can format the text that a user enters into the form. See Chapter 3, #18, "Text Formatting with Class Styles," for a discussion on how to create and apply Custom class styles.

Radio Buttons vs. Check Boxes

Radio buttons (aka option buttons) and check boxes represent two different ways to allow visitors to make selections from a set of options in a form. Radio buttons force a visitor to choose just one from a set of options.

(continued on next page)

One frequently encountered situation in which radio buttons are the best way to collect information is when you are collecting credit card information from a purchaser. In that case, you want him or her to select one, and just one, type of card from a list of cards you accept.

On the other hand, check boxes (aka option boxes) allow visitors to choose, or not choose, any number of options. For instance, you might ask those filling out a form if they want to be contacted by email, phone, snail mail, or text messaging. If you want to allow them to choose any combination of these options (including all or none of them), use check boxes.

How Radio Buttons Are Generated

Among the advantages of using Dreamweaver's Label dialog is that accessible labels are generated along with the radio button group and individual radio button values. There is no need for a distinct process of defining accessibility options for radio button groups if you use Dreamweaver's radio button group feature.

2. In the Name field, enter a name that indicates *to you* the nature of the group of options. For example, if you are inquiring as to a type of shipping (Overnight, Two-day, Ground, etc.), you might call your group "Shipping_options."

3. In the Radio buttons area of the dialog, click the Label column. In the first row enter a label that will appear for visitors. Next to that label, in the Value column, enter the data that will be sent with the form. For example, a label might read "Two-day shipping" to make clear to users what they are selecting. But the value sent to your shipping department might be "TD-002"—an internal code that tells those in the department how to handle and bill shipping.

4. In the second row, enter another label and value. Use the plus button to add more rows of labels and values and the minus button to delete a selected row. Use the Up and Down arrow buttons to move selected rows up or down in the list of radio buttons.

5. In the "Lay out using" area, choose either the Line breaks radio button (for separated rows) or the Table radio button (for rows designed in a table).

6. After you define the radio button options, click OK in the dialog to generate the radio button group.

After you generate a radio button group, you can edit (or delete) radio buttons individually. If you want to add a radio button, you can copy and paste an existing one from the group and, in the Properties inspector, change the Checked value (but not the Radio Button) content.

Menus and file fields are two different types of fields that can be placed in forms. Menus allow visitors to choose from a list of items. File fields allow users to upload files when they submit a form. In this how-to, you'll explore both types of fields. (Consider this two how-tos for the price of one—I had to sneak them both into the same one to keep the book at an even 100 how-tos!)

Menus (sometimes called pop-up menus) allow visitors to choose one option from a pop-up menu. The main difference between menus and list menus is that list menus allow users to select more than one choice from a list, whereas regular menus restrict users to choosing just one item. List menus are usually a confusing way to collect data and are rarely used.

To create a menu, follow these steps:

1. With your cursor inside an existing form, choose Insert > Form > Select (List/Menu). You use this menu option to create *either* a menu or a list menu. Later, you will decide whether to make your menu a list menu or a regular menu.

2. To create a list for the menu, click the List Values button in the Properties inspector. The List Values dialog appears. In the Item Label column, enter the text that will display in the menu (for example, **Alaska**). In the Value column, enter the value that will be collected and sent in the form (such as **AK**). Use the plus button to add new items to the list and the minus button to delete selected items. After you define the list, click OK (**Figure 26d**).

List Values		
Item Label	**Value**	
Choose a city...		
New York City	NYC	
Oakland	OAK	
Webster	WEB	
Minneapolis	MPL	
Fargo	FGO	

Figure 26d Defining list values.

3. After you generate a menu (or list), use the Properties inspector to define additional features. If you click the List option button in the Type area of the Properties inspector, you can convert the menu into a list menu. If you choose the List option, you can click the Allow Multiple check box in the Options area of the Properties inspector to allow users to choose more than one option from the menu. List menus can also display more than one option at a time in the drop-down menu.

4. You can add, delete, or edit actual menu (or list) items by clicking the List Values button in the Properties inspector. This will open the List Values dialog, where you can edit or change the order of menu (or list) options. You can change the initially selected option in the Properties

(continued on next page)

Radio Button Group Names

Why don't you change the Radio Button information when you edit radio buttons? Because the Radio Button value defines the *group*. The values of individual radio buttons within a group can change, but the group name must be the same for all buttons in the group. You can test your radio button group in a browser or Live view; if you choose one option from within the group, all other options should become deselected. If that doesn't happen, you haven't assigned the exact same group name (in the Radio Button field in the Properties inspector) to each radio button.

Because radio buttons are organized into groups, they are a little more complicated to define than other form fields. And because Dreamweaver is the ultimate Web design program, it includes a dialog (Radio Group) that manages the whole process of defining a radio button group easily.

What's Wrong with List Menus That Allow Multiple Options?

Pop-up menus are intuitive. Everyone is familiar with them, and they are easy to use. List menus, on the other hand, can be annoying. To choose multiple items, you must Command-click (Mac) or Ctrl-click (Windows). Add to this the fact that in a long list menu it's hard to tell which options have been selected and which ones have not. For these reasons, list menus are not a good way to have visitors choose multiple items. Instead, consider check boxes—an intuitive, clear way for users to choose one or more options from a list.

Don't Limit Filename Sizes

Don't constrain the number of characters that visitors can use to define an uploaded file by entering a value in the Max chars field in the Properties inspector. There is no point to setting a limit on the number of characters in an uploaded file's name.

inspector by clicking an option in the Initially selected area. You can assign a CSS style using the Class pop-up menu.

Note

The Properties inspector must be expanded to see the initially selected option.

File field forms allow visitors to attach files from their own computers to the form and send them along with the form. You can allow visitors to attach files to the form submission by inserting a File field in a form. Choose Insert > Form > File Field. You can define character width in the Properties inspector. A Browse button appears next to the field that the user can use to navigate to and select a file to upload.

For form content to be sent to a server, there must be a Submit button in the form. Submit buttons are usually matched with a Reset button. The Reset button clears any data entered into the form and allows the user to start fresh.

To place a button in a form, choose Insert > Form > Button. Use the Properties inspector to define the button as a Submit or Reset button. In the Action area, choose the Submit form or Reset form radio button (**Figure 26e**).

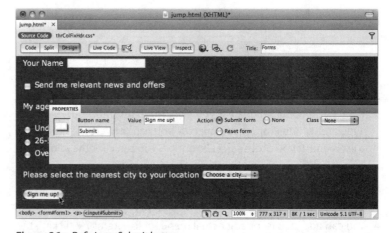

Figure 26e Defining a Submit button.

You can define custom labels for either the Submit or Reset button by entering text in the Value field for either button. Don't get too fancy; visitors are used to seeing buttons that display something like Submit or Reset. But if you enter different text in the Value field, that text will display in browsers and can be previewed in the Document window.

Using Hidden Fields

Hidden fields send information to a server that is not entered by the visitor filling out the online form. Hidden fields can be used to identify things like the page from which a form was sent. Normally, you won't be creating hidden fields. It's more likely that they will be included in the HTML for a form that you download, connected to an existing server script. If you do need to create a hidden field in a form, choose Insert > Form > Hidden Field. The field, of course, does not display in the form; it appears only as an icon in the Document window. Enter a name for the field in the Hidden-Field field in the Properties inspector and enter a value in the Value field.

Submit Buttons Are Essential!

No other settings are usually applied to Submit or Reset buttons, but a Submit button is essential if the form content is to be sent to a server.

#27 Testing Input with Validation Scripts

Testing Data with Scripts

Many times you will want to test content entered into a text field before you allow a visitor to submit the form. For example, you might require visitors to enter their name before submitting a form. In that case, the validation test would be that a visitor could not leave the Name field blank before submitting it. The Spry Validation Text Field widget can detect a blank field and alert the person filling out the form that a name is required before the form can be submitted. Or, you might want to test content entered into a text field even beyond determining whether or not the field was left blank. If, for example, you are collecting a zip code from the visitor, you can test to see if the data entered into the zip code field actually is a five- or nine-digit zip code. You can use the Spry Validation Text Field widget to verify that the data submitted in the form field conforms to the criteria you define, and again, force people to provide data that at least looks like a zip code before the form can be submitted.

Spry tools in Dreamweaver CS5 make it easy to define forms with attached validation scripts. These scripts test form content before it is submitted to make sure certain rules are met; specifically in the case of the new Spry form fields, they require that a visitor fill in a form field before submitting the form.

For example, if you want to require that visitors fill in the Email Address field in a form before they submit it, you can place a Spry Validation Text Field in your form. The four how-tos in this chapter explain how to use these Spry validation widgets.

All Spry validation widgets generate JavaScript to allow a form field to test input before processing the form. They also generate new CSS files that contain the formatting that defines the color, background color, text format, and so on for the form field and for form field input.

To place a Spry Validation Text Field widget in a form, follow these steps:

1. *Within a form,* select Insert > Spry > Spry Validation Text Field.

2. A text field appears in your form. With the new text field selected, the Spry text field options are displayed in the Properties inspector.

3. In the Spry Text Field box in the Properties inspector, enter a field name with no spaces or special characters (use alphanumeric characters). The field name is used to process data and is not displayed in a browser.

4. By default, the Required check box is selected in the Properties inspector. Leave this check box selected to make the text field a required field.

5. If you want to test data entered into the text field to meet validation criteria (for instance, the data must be in the form of an email address, a zip code, a URL, or a phone number), select one of those options from the Type pop-up menu in the Properties inspector (**Figure 27a**).

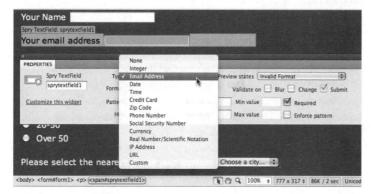

Figure 27a Choosing Email Address as the validation type.

6. The Enforce Pattern check box makes it impossible for users to enter characters that do not conform to the validation rule. For example, if you define validation rules for a U.S. zip code and a user tries to enter a letter (like A), that character will not appear in the field.

7. Use the Hint box in the Properties inspector to provide initial content in the text field (for instance, you might use **youremail@email.com** to suggest to users that they need to enter a complete email address).

8. Choose when to validate the field entry from the set of Validate on check boxes. Use Blur to validate when a user clicks outside the text field. Select Change to validate as the user changes text inside the text field. Choosing Submit validates when the user clicks the Submit button in the form.

9. The Preview States pop-up menu in the Properties inspector just defines what state is displayed in the Document window in Dreamweaver. The state that displays in a browser depends on whether the user conforms to or breaks the validation rules.

Including Options or Rules for Preset Validation Types

For example, if you chose to test input for zip codes, you can test for five-digit (US-5), nine-digit (US-9), British (UK), or Canadian (Canada) format. The Format pop-up menu displays these options. Many of the preset validation types include rules defining how many characters will be allowed and/or maximum and minimum values. For example, the five-digit zip code validation type will only accept five numbers.

Creating Your Own Validation Rules

You can create your own validation rules for text boxes by choosing Integer (number) from the Type pop-up menu in the Properties inspector, and then defining a maximum (Max chars) and/or minimum (Min chars) number of characters, and a maximum (Max value) and/or minimum (Min value) value for numbers entered into the field.

You can edit Spry validation rules at any time by selecting the turquoise Spry Text Field label and changing values in the Properties inspector.

Although validation scripts are most widely used for text boxes, they can be defined (in a way similar to the steps I just outlined for text boxes) for other form fields as well.

Spry Validation Text Field Widgets Don't Verify Actual Data

To be clear: None of the Spry Validation Text Field widgets actually looks up data and verifies that it is accurate. But the widgets do verify that at least the correct form of data has been submitted, eliminating forms that are sent to your server that don't have required information fields filled in.

Validating Text Area Input?

Text area fields are used almost exclusively for comments—and comments in this digital age are one of the more available ways that customers, clients, students, patients, and people in general communicate with organizations and businesses. If you place a text area field in a form, you might well want to use the Spry Validation TextArea widget to define a few rules for how much content can be entered in the field.

Validating Checkbox Input?

Sometimes a check box provides an option that a user can either choose or not choose. Do you want to receive unsolicited email? Do you have a discount code? Did you hear about this Web site from a friend? In all these cases, a form designer will likely allow the user to select, or not, any or all of the check boxes. In other cases, clicking a check box is mandatory to submit a form. Required check boxes are used to verify that a visitor has read a license agreement before downloading software or that a visitor agrees to set terms before reading site content.

#28 Connecting a Form to a Server Script

Form actions define how the data in a form is sent to a database on a server. Form actions are defined in the Properties inspector with the *form*—not any specific form field—selected.

Tip
To select a form, click the dashed red line defining the form border. Or, click the <form> tag in the tag selector area on the bottom of the Document window.

The three important fields in the Properties inspector for a form are the Action, Method, and Enctype fields. What you enter in these fields is determined by how the programmer (who set up the script and database to which the form data is being sent) configured the database and scripts at the server. Normally, Method is usually set to POST but can sometimes be set to GET; this again depends on how data is transferred to the server and is defined by how the server is configured. The Action field contains the URL of the Web page at the server that has the script that will manage the data.

Enctype, short for "encryption type," is sometimes used to define how characters are interpreted and formatted. Your server administrator will tell you what, if any, enctype coding is required for forms to be processed by your server.

Because form actions are determined by the settings at your server, the information you enter into the Properties inspector is provided by your server administrator. In the case of forms designed to match server scripts, those forms normally come with Action settings defined.

If you want to collect data in a form and have it sent to an email address, you can do this easily without having to work with additional server configuration or scripts. In the Action field, type **mailto:**<*your email address*>. From the Method pop-up menu, choose POST. In the Enctype field, type **text/plain** (**Figure 28a**).

Figure 28a Defining an action that will send form content to an email address—in this case, mine!

Let me give you a recipe for one of the most widely used server-connected forms: a search engine. Follow these steps to place a FreeFind

Online CGI Services

Many online services provide you with server-side databases and scripts, and these services often host online databases and scripts as well (or they tell you how to copy them to your server). For example, there are services that allow you to host a mailing list at their server. They provide you with HTML that you copy into your Web page. That HTML contains the coding for the form, as well as a connection to a script at a server that manages the data put into the form.

Helpful CGI Scripts, Forms, and Hosting Services

In addition to the FreeFind search service, there are a few other useful sources for scripts and hosting to manage form data. These sites provide various sets of available forms and scripts that collect Web statistics, collect feedback, manage message boards, generate survey polls, allow guestbook listings,

(continued on next page)

search field on an open Dreamweaver Web page. You can also use them as a model for using similar services.

1. Go to www.freefind.com and enter your email address and your site's URL (at an online server). Click the Instant Signup button. FreeFind emails you a password, a login, and a link to the FreeFind control center. Follow the link, log in, and then click the link for a free search field (or you can choose one of the more elaborate, ad-free pay options).

2. Click the Build Index tab in the FreeFind control center, and then click the Index Now link. FreeFind builds a database at the FreeFind server of all the words in your Web site.

3. Click the HTML tab and choose one of the four available types of search field forms you can use (the options are Site Search Only, Site and Web Search, Web Search Only, or Text Links).

4. Select all the HTML for the search field you selected, and choose Edit > Copy from your browser menu.

5. Back in Dreamweaver, click in the Document window to set the place where the search field will be inserted. Then choose View > Code to switch to Code view. Don't worry about any of the code you see—your cursor is in the spot you clicked in Design view. Choose Edit > Paste to place the HTML code and switch back to Design view to see the search field (**Figure 28b**).

Note
The form copied from FreeFind includes hidden fields, which are indicated by icons in the form. These fields have information that directs search queries to the index FreeFind prepares for your particular site.

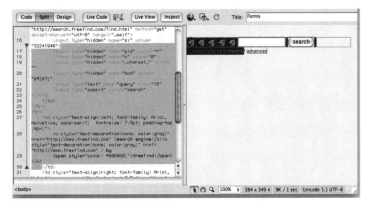

Figure 28b Placing a search field from FreeFind.

Test your search field in a browser. The search field form has fields and buttons. You can reformat the fields and buttons using the techniques for defining form and form field attributes we've covered. In other words, you can customize the way this form looks—you just can't delete any of the form fields. Other techniques in this chapter cover how customization works, so you can customize forms you get from CGI hosts.

and store and manage email lists. You can find online database and script services by searching for "CGI scripts." CGI stands for Common Gateway Interface and is the protocol (system) that is used (with options for various programming languages) to manage form input.

Can't See Your Form in Dreamweaver?

Normally, forms display in the Document window (in Design view) as red lines. This border is invisible in a browser. Dreamweaver displays the borders of forms as a highly helpful tool so that you can make sure all your form fields are inside your form. If they're not inside the form, they won't work.

Displaying form outlines is a default option that you can turn off. If you don't see the dashed red line indicating the form, turn on this option by choosing View > Visual Aids > Invisible Elements. With Invisible Elements selected in this submenu, you'll be able to see your form.

CHAPTER FIVE

Adding Effects and Interactivity with Spry and JavaScript

JavaScript programming works with CSS styles to enable animation and interactivity in Web sites. Here are some examples: A visitor scrolls over an area of the page, and another area of the page changes to display new content; a visitor clicks on a menu, and a submenu opens up; or a panel expands and collapses on a mouse click.

You'll learn to generate all three of those interactive elements in this chapter, and through the course of being introduced to various examples, you'll learn the method and system for enabling interactivity in your Web site.

Dreamweaver CS5 incorporates a set of animation and interactivity tools that use the Ajax set of tools. Ajax applications generate animation or interactivity by combining and assigning attributes to HTML (Web-page coding), CSS (style sheets), and JavaScript (which is generated by Dreamweaver).

Before diving into Ajax-based interactivity and animation, I'll expose you to an interesting way to embed live data in a Web page. Live data is data supplied by an external source and displayed in a Web page. This is in contrast to static Web pages, where the content is actually in the page itself. Dreamweaver CS5 makes a lightweight but accessible and useful version of live data available through Spry Data displays. These displays present data from an HTML table saved at a separate Web page.

And, so, in the course of this chapter, you'll also learn how to create a basic table. Tables were originally developed for presenting data in rows and columns on Web pages. Later, they evolved into an awkward but widely implemented technique for laying out pages. Today, CSS styles have replaced tables as the standard technique for page design, but tables are still useful for storing data (for a full exploration of page design with CSS, see Chapter 2, "Designing Web Pages in Dreamweaver with CSS Styles").

#29 Creating a Spry Data Source Table

Use a Spry Data Source for...

You might want to use a Spry data source table for the following:

- An updated product and price list
- An updated company directory
- An updated photo portfolio
- A customer support database with a list of questions and answers

The easiest and most accessible way to create a Spry data source is to define and populate a table that lists all the information you want to display in the Spry data display. The Spry data display you generate on a separate Web page will be attractive and accessible. The Spry data display table does not have to be attractive because it will only be seen and used by whoever updates it.

Data tables are generally organized into *columns* that reflect *fields* and *rows* that reflect specific items (referred to as "records" in database terminology). So, for example, a product database might include *fields* like Item, Price, Description, and Image (the last being a photo of the product). In such a table, each *row* would hold information for a specific product.

To create a Spry data source table, follow these steps:

1. Create a new HTML page (choose File > New to open the New Document dialog, choose Blank Page from the category list on the left, choose HTML / None as the page type, and click Create).

2. Save the page (assign a filename like **data01.html** to help you remember that this is the page that holds your Spry data source table).

3. Choose Insert > Table to open the Table dialog. In the Columns box, enter the number of *fields* (columns) required to organize your data.

4. Leave the Rows box set to the default number. You can easily add rows to your table as you enter new items into it.

5. Leave the Border set to 1.

6. Set Table Width to 100% to create the most convenient layout to enter data.

7. Set Cell Padding to 6 to make the table data more readable (cell padding provides a buffer between the different rows and columns of data).

8. In the Header area of the dialog, select Top. This provides automatic formatting for your column headings.

9. You can enter a caption to improve accessibility if the table will be used by people with visual handicaps.

10. After you complete the Table dialog (**Figure 29a**), click OK to generate the table.

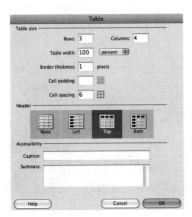

Figure 29a Defining a table to use as a Spry data source.

11. With the table generated, enter column headings (field names) in the top row of the table.

12. Populate the Spry data source table with information for your database. Use a separate row for each item.

(continued on next page)

Inserting or Deleting Rows

At any time you can edit the content of the Spry data source table by deleting data or entering new data. To insert or delete a row, Control-click (Mac) or right-click (Windows) and choose Table > Insert Row or Table > Delete Row from the context menu.

13. The last and important step in creating a Spry data source table is to name the table using the Table box in the Properties inspector. To do this, select the table by clicking on the table border. In the Table box, enter a name for your table. Avoid spaces or nonalphanumeric characters (**Figure 29b**).

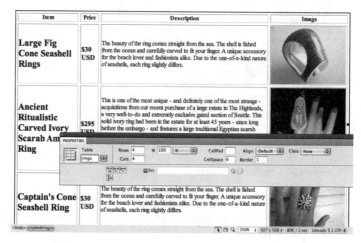

Figure 29b Data table with field names, data, and a table name.

#**30** Generating a Spry Data Display

You can insert a Spry data display in any existing Web page, or you can create a new Web page and use the entire page to display the Spry data display. The only trick is that you must have first created a Spry data source (if you haven't done that, jump back to #29, "Creating a Spry Data Source Table").

To generate the Spry data display, follow these steps:

1. Choose Insert > Spry > Spry Data Set. The Spry Data Set wizard launches.

2. In the Select Data Type pop-up menu, choose HTML.

3. Click the Browse button in the Specify Data File area and navigate to and select the file you created with the Spry data source table. Your data table displays in the preview area.

4. From the Data Containers pop-up menu, choose the specific table with your data (**Figure 30a**).

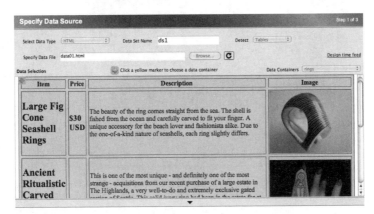

Figure 30a Choosing a data table to embed as a Spry data display.

5. With the data source defined, click the Next button in the Spry Data Set wizard. Normally, there is no reason to change the default options in step 2 of the wizard. However, if you are comfortable with database management concepts, you can use the Type pop-up menu to change the way data is recognized, and you can sort rows. After examining the settings in step 2, click Next.

(continued on next page)

6. The final step in the Spry Data Set wizard allows you to choose from four different layouts to display your data. Each layout option includes a thumbnail illustration and a description. Choose one of the layout options. (The fifth option, Do Not Insert HTML, voids the whole point of the wizard and is for programmers who want to define custom data presentation.)

7. With a layout selected, click the Set Up button associated with your choice. Each layout includes customized and different Set Up options, but they all boil down to the ability to add, delete, or change the order of display of columns. Use the Add, Delete, Up, and Down arrows to adjust the displays (**Figure 30b**).

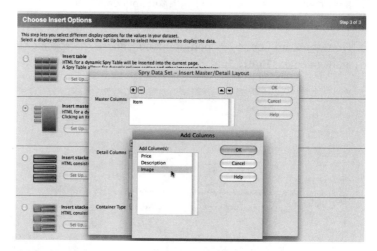

Figure 30b Adding a column to the Master Column display in the Insert Master/Detail Layout.

8. After adjusting layout options, if desired, click Done in the Spry Data Set wizard to generate the Spry Data Set layout.

Adding Effects and Interactivity with Spry and JavaScript

You can preview the Spry Data display in Live view: choose View > Live View (**Figure 30c**).

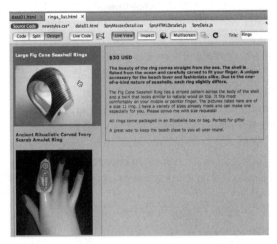

Figure 30c Previewing a Spry Data display in Live view.

Updating a Spry Data Source

It's easy to update the data in a Spry data source. When you open the Web page with your Spry data source table, you can simply add, edit, or delete data. As you save the page with the Spry data source table, the data displayed in the Spry data display (on a separate Web page) updates automatically.

Why Isn't There an Easier Way to Revise a Spry Data Display?

There is no nice, easy way to reopen the Spry Data Set wizard and change display settings. If you want to substantially revise your Spry data display layout, the best way to do that is to delete your existing layout and go through the wizard again! Why? Spry data displays involve a large number of generated CSS objects for page layout. Those CSS objects are very different for each of the four layouts (and layout options make the differences even more complex). Given all that, it doesn't take that long and it's pretty simple to redefine a *new* Spry data display if you want to change your data display layout.

#31 Generating and Formatting Spry Menu Bars

Deleting a Spry Widget

To select (and then delete) a Spry widget in Design view of the Document window:

1. Click on the border of the widget or the widget label that appears at the top-left corner of the widget when you hover over that spot to select the widget.

2. Press the Delete key to remove the widget from your page.

Remember: Save Before You Spry

Before you create any Spry widgets, make sure you save the Web page you are working on.

What Are the Div Tags for Widgets?

Widget div tag names vary depending on the particular widget and how many of that particular widget you have on a page. But the div tags all begin with "div" followed by the name of the particular widget. For example, the tag for a menu bar is MenuBar# (with # representing the number of menu bars on the page).

Menu bars, which display submenus when they are hovered over, are a useful and appealing page element. Menu bars allow several menu options to be accessed from a clean, uncluttered main menu. The interactivity they provide when a visitor hovers over a menu option adds energy and dynamism to your page.

The Spry widget for inserting Menu Bar widgets allows you to generate menu bars with two levels of submenus. That means a user can click on a menu option that will in turn reveal a submenu with a new set of options, choose one of those options, and pick from yet a second submenu.

To generate a Menu Bar widget, you must first save the page in which you plan to insert the widget. Then choose Insert > Spry> Spry Menu Bar. The Spry Menu Bar dialog appears, and you can choose between a horizontal or vertical menu bar. Click OK in the Spry Menu Bar dialog to generate the Menu Bar widget.

The menu bar that is generated is generic with four menu items (Item 1, Item 2, Item 3, and Item 4). You can customize basic menu bar properties like the display menu name and the link target in the Properties inspector.

To edit the content and links for a selected menu bar, choose menu items (initially labeled Item 1, Item 2, etc.) or submenu items (initially labeled Item 1.1, Item 1.2, etc.) in the Properties inspector.

With an item (or subitem) selected, you can enter text in the active Text field of the Properties inspector that will appear in the menu. In the Link box, you can enter the link that will open when the item is clicked.

Use the Title box in the Properties inspector to enter accessibility text (this text will appear in a browser window when a user hovers over the menu option). Leave the Target box blank to open the link in the same browser window or enter **_blank** to open the link in a new browser window.

Adding Effects and Interactivity with Spry and JavaScript

You can use the plus and minus icons above the menu or submenu (or sub-submenu) columns to add or delete new menu items. Use the Move Item Up or Move Item Down icon to change the order of menu items (**Figure 31a**).

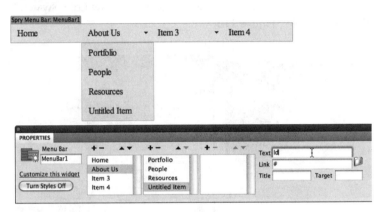

Figure 31a The Properties inspector for menu bars.

To edit the styles associated with a Menu Bar widget, expand the menu bar style sheet in the CSS Styles panel. This style sheet will be named SpryMenuBarHorizontal.css, or SpryMenuBarVertical.css if you created a vertical menu bar. Every menu bar generates at least a dozen CSS styles. Selecting one of these Class styles in the top part of the CSS Styles panel allows you to edit properties for that style in the bottom half of the CSS Styles panel.

Turn Styles Off Button?

When you select a Menu Bar widget (or as you create one), you will notice a Turn Styles Off button in the Properties inspector. Turning styles off does not affect how the style is rendered in a browser, but it turns off formatting in the Document window (essentially reducing your menu bar to an outline in the Document window). You can adjust the formatting of different menu bar properties of a selected menu bar in the CSS Styles panel. Some of the CSS Style options control relatively inconspicuous elements of the menu bar, but all of them can be edited in the CSS Styles panel.

Horizontal or Vertical Menu Bars?

Menu Bar widgets can be horizontal or vertical. Vertical menu bars typically are aligned in a frame, table column, or other layout objects (like a div or an AP div) on the left side of the page. Horizontal menu bars are typically aligned on the top of the page and can be placed there without being inserted in a layout object.

What Are All Those Menu Bar Styles About?

Most of the CSS styles that are generated to format your Menu Bar widget define the positioning and size of the menus and submenus that appear when a user hovers over a menu option. The default positioning of these menus is usually fine and does not need to be adjusted. You can customize a unique menu bar by creating your own links and text, and you can create a distinctive format by customizing text and background colors, hover styles, padding, and so on.

To change the background or text color for the menu bar, select the style ul.MenuBarHorizontal a (or for a vertical menu bar, select the style ul.MenuBarVertical a). With the style selected in the CSS Styles panel, use the background-color swatch box in the bottom half of the CSS Styles panel to choose a new background color and use the Color swatch to change font color (**Figure 31b**).

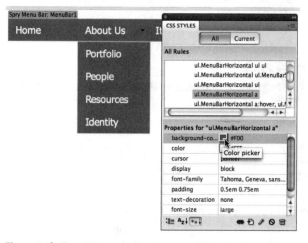

Figure 31b Examining and editing menu styles in the CSS Styles panel.

When you save the page in which the Spry menu bar is embedded, the style sheet file associated with the menu bar updates. Test your Spry menu bar in Live view.

#32 Defining and Populating Spry Tabbed Panels

Tabbed panels transform a single Web page into a series of tabbed panels that look like distinct Web pages to a visitor. Tabbed panels are one way to create an easily navigable Web site. To create a set of tabbed panels for an open Web page, choose Insert > Spry > Tabbed Panels. A generic set of two tabbed panels appears in the Document window. Save your page—always required before inserting Spry widgets.

To change the title of a tab, click on the tab and enter a new name. To enter content in a tabbed panel, click a tab. The selected tab displays a blue outline. Click in the Content area below the tab and enter content for that tab. Tab content can be anything you would place on a regular Web page, including text and images (**Figure 32a**).

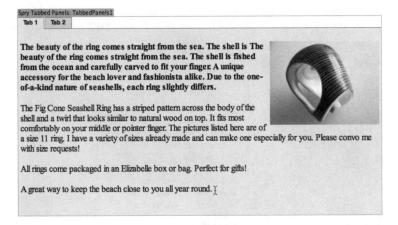

Figure 32a Entering content into a tabbed panel.

You can add (or delete) tabbed panels for a selected tabbed panel in the Properties inspector. To select an *entire tabbed panel* as opposed to a single tab, click the border of the entire tabbed panel. When you do this, the Tabbed Panels Properties inspector allows you to add panels by clicking the plus icon in the Panels section of the Properties inspector.

To change the name of a tabbed panel, double-click the current label (for example, Tab 1) and type a new label.

Deleting Tabbed Panels

You can delete a tabbed panel by selecting it in the Properties inspector and clicking the minus icon in the Panels area. Also, you can move a selected tabbed panel up or down in the Properties inspector using the Up and Down triangles in the Panels area. Moving a selected panel up moves that panel to the left in the tabbed panel order.

Visibility

When you hover over a tabbed panel, you will see an eye icon. Clicking the eye icon displays the tabbed panel content.

Using the CSS Styles Panel to Format Tabbed Panels

You can change the background color of tabbed panel elements in the CSS Styles panel:

- To change the background color for a hovered-over tab, choose the .Tabbed PanelsTabHover style in the CSS Styles panel, and then choose a background color from the background-color property.

- To change the background color for a selected tab, choose the .TabbedPanels TabSelected style in the CSS Styles panel, and then choose a background color from the background-color property.

- To change the background color for a tabbed content area, select that tab in the Document window, choose the .Tabbed PanelsContentGroup style in the CSS Styles panel, and then choose a background color from the background-color property.

Format the content of tabbed panels the same way you format text or images.

To format elements of the tab like background and text color, select the CSS Styles panel (choose Window > CSS Styles) and view the styles for SpryTabbedPanels.css. When you expand this CSS file in the CSS Styles panel, a set of Class styles appears in the CSS Styles panel. In the lower part of the CSS Styles panel, you can change the properties of any style you select in the top part of the panel. The sidebar "Using the CSS Styles Panel to Format Tabbed Panels" explains how to edit frequently changed elements of a panel style. Feel free to experiment with other properties.

For example, to change background color for nonselected tabs, click the .Tabbed PanelsTab style in the CSS Styles panel, and then choose a background color from the background-color property (**Figure 32b**).

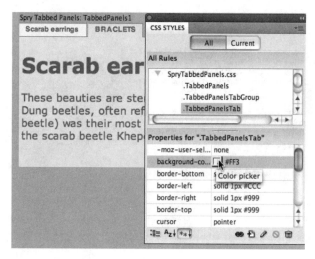

Figure 32b Changing the background color for nonselected tabs.

#**33** Creating Collapsible Panels

Spry collapsible panels are handy ways to present optional information in a Web page. These panels have a clickable tab and a content area that displays or hides when a visitor clicks the tab.

The Web page that I use to check my bank balance, for example, has a number of clickable spots on the page where I can get explanations for terms or see additional detail. This information might not be necessary for a visitor and would in many cases clutter the page. But when presented in a collapsible panel, such information is handy but doesn't take up space.

To insert a Spry collapsible panel, first save your page, and then choose Insert > Spry > Spry Collapsible Panel. In the Document window, click and drag to select the default text, "tab," and enter a new label for the collapsible panel. Visitors will see this label in their browser window. Clicking this tab label in a browser toggles between displaying and hiding the panel. In the Content area of the collapsible panel, delete the "Content" default text and enter new page content. That page content can be anything you would put on a regular Web page.

When you create or select a
Spry collapsible panel, the
Properties inspector has two
menus: Display and Default
State. If you choose Open
from the Display menu, the
collapsible panel is always
open in the Document win-
dow. Independently of that,
you can choose either Open
or Closed from the Default
State menu. If you choose
Open, which is the default,
the Spry collapsible panel is
open when a visitor opens
your Web page and only collapses if he or she clicks the
tab. In my opinion, this basically defeats the purpose of
a collapsible panel, and most
of the time you will want
to choose Closed from the
Default State menu.

As you can with other Spry widgets, you can edit basic features of
the Collapsible Panel widget in the Properties inspector (see the sidebar
"Hide or Display Spry Collapsible Panels?"). To format elements of the widget like background and text color, select the CSS Styles panel (choose
Window > CSS Styles) and view the styles for the SpryCollapsiblePanel.css
sheet by expanding that style sheet. The main property of a collapsible
panel that you will need to edit in the CSS Styles panel is the background
color for the tab. You can edit the actual tab text in Design view, but to
edit the background of the collapsible panel tab, edit the background-
color property of the .CollapsiblePanelTab style (**Figure 33a**).

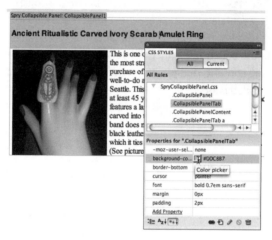

Figure 33a Formatting the background of a Spry
collapsible panel.

#34 Defining Spry Tooltips

Spry tooltips generate pop-up text that appears when a visitor hovers over an image or selected text on a Web page. To create a Spry tooltip, click to place your cursor at an insertion point where the tooltip text will appear (don't type the tooltip trigger text first; creating the trigger text is part of the Tooltip properties that you define later).

With an image selected, or your text insertion point where the trigger text for the tooltip will appear, choose Insert > Spry > Spry Tooltip. A box with some default text appears. Replace the text "Tooltip trigger goes here" with the text that you want to trigger the tooltip. Replace the text that says "Tooltip content goes here" with the text that will appear in the tooltip (**Figure 34a**).

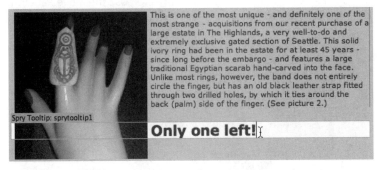

Figure 34a Previewing tooltip content.

Tooltip properties usually are fine without changing the default settings, but they can be adjusted in the Properties inspector. The Horizontal and Vertical Offset boxes define how far to offset the tooltip text (to the right and down, respectively). The Show Delay and Hide Delay boxes allow you to enter values (in seconds) for how long you want to wait to display tooltip text after the trigger text is hovered over and how long to wait after the trigger text is no longer hovered over to hide the tooltip.

The Blind and Fade options generate effects that are not appropriate for displaying useful, readable tooltip text, and the Hide on Mouse Out check box is not operative. The Follow mouse check box moves tooltip text as a user's mouse moves within the trigger text.

#35 Inserting a Spry Accordion Widget

Formatting Spry Accordion Panels

View the styles associated with the Spry accordion in the CSS Styles panel. The CSS file with the styles for the Accordion widget is Spry-Accordion.css. Select and expand that style in the CSS Styles panel to see the class styles associated with your accordion panel.

- To format the tab background color for non-selected tabs, edit the background-color property in the .Accordion-PanelTab style. For the selected tab, edit the .AccordionPanel Open .Accordion PanelTab style.

- To change the text color that displays when a user hovers over a tab for an unopened accordion panel, edit the color property of the .Accor-dionPanel TabHover style. For an opened accordion panel, edit the .AccordionPanelOpen .AccordionPanel Tab-Hover style.

Spry Accordion widgets are one more interactive, dynamic way to make a page with a lot of content more inviting. The widget creates horizontal regions on a Web page that can be expanded or collapsed (just one is expanded at any one time).

To insert a Spry accordion, first save your page, and then choose Insert > Spry > Accordion. By default, a two-part accordion is created with Label 1 and Content 1 on top, and Label 2 and Content 2 on the bottom. Click and drag to select the default text ("Label 1") and insert your own. This is what visitors will see before they expand the accordion. In the Content area, enter anything you might include in a normal full Web page.

To add or delete Spry accordion sections, use the Add Panel or Remove Panel icon in the Properties inspector. Use the Move Panel Up list and Move Panel Down List icons to rearrange the order of your panels (**Figure 35a**).

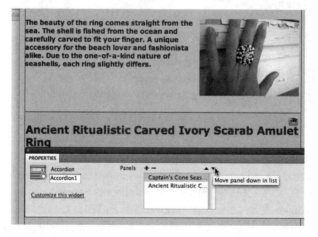

Figure 35a Moving a Spry accordion panel down in the list in the Properties inspector.

#36 Opening a Browser Window with JavaScript

They're often called pop-ups—those little browser windows that open when you load a page in your browser or when you activate the window by some action on the Web page. In Dreamweaver's terminology, they are referred to as *browser windows*, which is actually an accurate description of what most people call pop-ups.

With the Web page that will open in a new browser window prepared and saved (see the sidebar "Before You Start"), follow these steps to define the window:

1. In the tag bar, at the bottom of Design view, select the <body> tag. From the Behaviors panel, click the plus button and choose Open Browser Window from the list of behaviors.

2. In the "URL to display" field, navigate to or enter the Web page that will open in the new browser window.

3. Use the Window width and Window height fields to define the size of the browser window. The display options available in the Attributes section of the Open Browser Window dialog are generally *not* enabled—the new browser window that pops up is usually displayed without features like a navigation toolbar or status bar. So, leave these options deselected (**Figure 36a**).

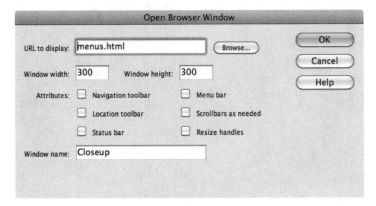

Figure 36a Defining pop-up browser window attributes.

4. Enter a name in the Window name field, and then click OK in the Open Browser Window dialog.

Before You Start

The first step in creating a behavior that will open a browser window is to create a special Web page that will appear in that browser window. Since this page is likely to be displayed in a small browser window (you will be defining the size of that browser window as part of the behavior), you should design a page that will work well in a small browser window.

Open Browser Window Triggers

Unless you have something on your page selected (like an image or a link), by default the open browser window behavior uses the page loading as the triggering event. In other words, the new browser window opens as soon as a visitor opens the launching page in his or her browser.

Test your new browser window behavior by opening the page that launches it in a browser.

You can change the triggering effect for a Behavior in the first column pop-up menu in the Behaviors panel (**Figure 36b**).

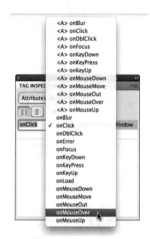

Figure 36b Defining onClick as the trigger to open a new browser window.

#37 Applying Effects

Effects like blinds, fades, or highlighting can be applied to almost any element on a Web page, including an image or a link.

Effects include the following:

- Appear/Fade makes the selected object appear or fade away.

- Blind creates a window blind-like effect that hides and reveals the object.

- Grow/Shrink makes the object bigger or smaller.

- Highlight changes the background color of the object.

- Shake moves the object from left to right.

- Slide moves the object up or down.

- Squish makes the object vanish into the upper-left corner of the page.

To apply an effect to a selected object, choose Effect from the Behaviors panel menu, and then choose one of the available effects (**Figure 37a**).

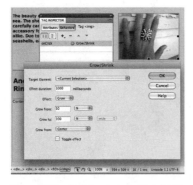

Figure 37a Defining a Grow/Shrink effect.

Each effect has its own dialog with its own features.

Deleting behaviors can be confusing and frustrating. This is one of the tasks my students most often call me over to their workstations to help them with. So, let me demystify that process.

Defining Elements for Effects

You may need to switch to Split view when you select text to which you apply an effect, to see exactly what elements have been selected for the effect.

Effect Settings

Each Dreamweaver effect has settings parameters. Some are pretty self-explanatory, like effect duration (which determines how long the effect lasts). Others are hard to explain. In reality, you'll experiment with various settings to see how the effect works in a browser.

Deleting a behavior involves two steps—finding the behavior in the Behaviors panel, and then deleting it. The first step is the hard part. The trick to locating a behavior in the Behaviors panel is to first select the object to which the behavior is associated. Only then will the behavior be easy to find in the Behaviors panel. Once you select the behavior in the Behaviors panel, click the minus (Remove Event) icon to delete the behavior.

What about events that are *not* attached to any object on a page but instead are attached to the actual page? These behaviors can be the hardest to find. But you can see them in the Behaviors panel if you click the <body> tag in the Tag Selector bar at the bottom of the Document window. Events that launch when a page is loaded or exited will likely be associated with the <body> tag.

Objects can have multiple behaviors attached to them. In that case, you must figure out which behavior you want to delete from the description in the Event (right) column of the Behaviors panel.

CHAPTER SIX

Embedding Media

As this book goes to press, online media standards are in a state of flux and a bit of turmoil. Adobe's Flash Player—which, as of this writing, is still widely established as the standard format for delivering video on the Web—is being challenged by new features in HTML5, supported by the new generation of browsers, that embed video without the Flash Player. So, in this chapter we'll explore both approaches, as well as techniques for embedding video using the HTML4 <EMBED> tag.

Which video format should you use? I can't make a call for you on that. All video formats have their strengths and weaknesses. Compressed and streaming video (like Flash Video [FLV]) cannot easily be downloaded or saved to a viewer's computer or mobile device, but it provides the highest-quality, fastest-downloading video available. QuickTime movies, on the other hand, may not download as quickly, but they can be easily configured and *can* be easily saved to a viewer's computer or mobile device.

Then there is the question of how to *package* your video. Dreamweaver CS5 makes it easy to embed FLV with a variety of player skins (controls and displays). MP4 videos (technically MP4 video can be packaged in FLVs, but here I'm referring to plain, "unwrapped" MP4s) can be embedded in Web pages using the new <AUDIO> and <VIDEO> tags in HTML5, and played on mobile devices like iPhones or iPads. I'll show you how to do that in the last How-To in this chapter.

In short, be flexible. Consider providing multiple (or at least a couple) video formats. In the next chapter, "Working with HTML5 Pack Extensions in Dreamweaver CS5," I'll explain how to use new tools available for Dreamweaver that allow you to preview and prepare content for multiple browsing environments.

Finally, in this chapter I've included an exploration of how to embed Flash (SWF) objects. These can be interactive elements like embedded games or forms, animation, graphical (and scalable) type, or any other object created in Flash.

#38 Embedding Flash (SWF)

SWF and FLV Are Different!

Despite the similar-sounding names, Flash movies (SWF files) and Flash Video (FLV files) are different things. Flash movies, often referred to as SWFs (often pronounced "swiffs"), present animated and interactive content online, and are created with Adobe's Flash authoring tool. The SWF format is also sometimes used to display digital artwork online.

When you embed a Flash (SWF) object in a Web page in Dreamweaver, you can adjust the size of the object, define the size and color of a background behind the object, and even adjust features like whether or not an animation plays automatically when the page in which it is inserted opens or if a visitor has to click a Play button.

To insert a SWF file into an open Web page, choose Insert > Media > SWF. If you have not saved the open document, Dreamweaver will prompt you to do so. After you choose Insert > Media > SWF, the Select File dialog appears. Navigate to a SWF file and click OK.

If you have selected accessibility prompts for SWF files in the Preferences dialog, you'll be prompted to enter a title for your SWF video. When you embed a SWF file in a Web page, the movie appears as a gray box. Clicking the Play button in the Properties inspector previews animation and/or enables interactivity built into the Flash (SWF) object (**Figure 38a**).

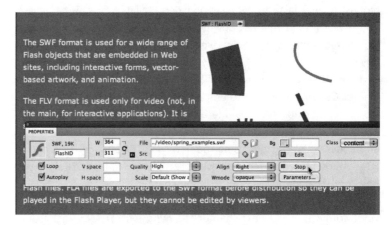

Figure 38a Previewing a Flash object with Play selected in the Properties inspector for a SWF movie.

You can adjust how the Flash Object displays and plays using parameters in the Properties Inspector:

- Use the Loop and AutoPlay check boxes to enable (or disable) looping (repeating) or autoplay (the animation plays when a page is loaded).

- The V Space and H Space fields allow you to define vertical (V) or horizontal (H) spacing between the Flash movie and other objects on the page.

- The Quality pop-up menu allows you to compress the Flash file (choose Low) for faster downloading and lower quality.

- In the Scale pop-up menu, the Default setting maintains the original height-to-width ratio of the original animation (that is, it prevents the animation from being distorted) when the Flash object is resized. The Exact Fit option in the Scale pop-up menu, on the other hand, allows you to stretch the animation horizontally or vertically if you change the original height and/or width.

- The Align pop-up menu is used to align the Flash object left or right, so text flows around the animation.

- The Bg pop-up menu is used to define a background color. The background color is active if you resize the Flash object and maintain the height-to-width aspect ratio by choosing the Default setting in the Scale field.

- The Reset size button restores the Flash object to its original size. The Edit button opens Flash (if you have it installed) to edit the Flash object.

- The Play button displays the Flash object in the Document window. Toggling to Stop displays the editable gray box.

- Selecting Transparent in the Wmode pop-up will make the background of the Flash object disappear if the background is a solid color.

FLV, SWF, and FLA— What's the Difference?

The SWF format is used for a wide range of Flash objects that are embedded in Web sites, including interactive forms, vector-based artwork, and animation. The FLV format is used only for video (not, in the main, for interactive applications). It is similar to the QuickTime or Windows Media formats. Both SWF and FLV files require that the Flash Player plug-in be installed in a viewer's browser. The FLA format is Flash's native file format and is used to save editable Flash files. FLA files are exported to the SWF format before distribution so they can be played in the Flash Player, but they cannot be edited by viewers.

#39 Embedding Flash Video (FLV)

How Accessible Are FLVs?

Flash files require the Adobe Flash Player, which is installed on a large percentage of computers and is also available as a free download (via www.adobe.com). Flash objects are not supported on iPhone, iPod Touch (or iPod), or iPad.

Embedding an FLV from YouTube?

YouTube (and as of this writing most other online video sources) present video in FLV format. To embed links to those videos (at the host server), most services like YouTube provide an "EMBED" link that generates HTML code for embedding their video into your Web page. Copy that HTML code and paste it into Code view in Dreamweaver CS5.

Adobe is successfully promoting the FLV format as a kind of "universal" video format that transcends other competing media formats. This is the video format used at YouTube.

Dreamweaver CS5 makes it easy to embed movies that have been saved to the FLV format, and then choose from a nice little set of player controls that display in a browser window to make it easy for visitors to control the movie.

To embed an FLV file, follow these steps:

1. Choose Insert > Media > FLV. The Insert FLV dialog opens. Use the Browse button to navigate to an FLV file (or enter the URL of a file on the Internet) in the URL field. Unless you are working with a special streaming server (and your server administrator will know this information), choose Progressive Download Video from the Video type pop-up menu.

2. Click the Detect Size button in the dialog to detect the size of the video. Keep the Constrain check box selected since it is unlikely that you will want to distort the height-to-width ratio of the video. You can enter a new value in either the Width or Height field to resize the video. If you selected the Constrain check box, the nonedited dimension will automatically adjust to keep the height-to-width ratio of the video the same as the original (**Figure 39a**).

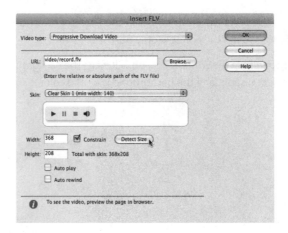

Figure 39a Embedding a Flash Video file with detected size.

3. After detecting the video size, you can use the Skin pop-up menu to select a player control set. Note that player controls require various sizes of videos, which is why you detected the video size in step 2 first (**Figure 39b**).

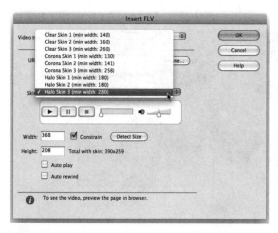

Figure 39b Choosing a Flash Player skin for an FLV video.

4. You can enable Auto play or Auto rewind, or prompt users to download Flash Player features if necessary, using the check boxes in the dialog. If you elect to prompt users to download the Flash Player, you can accept or edit the text message that displays.

The Auto play, Loop (Auto rewind), and size can be adjusted in the Properties inspector.

How Do You Create FLVs?

Adobe Video Encoder in CS5 transforms Windows Media or QuickTime videos into FLV format. For a complete, detailed, step-by-step guide to editing and generating FLVs and embedding FLV files in a Dreamweaver Web site, see *Enhancing a Dreamweaver CS3 Web Site with Flash Video: Visual QuickProject Guide* (Peachpit, 2008) by David Karlins.

Oddly enough, however, you cannot preview an FLV in Dreamweaver CS5's Live view. To preview your video, choose File > Preview in Browser, and choose a browser or device (**Figure 39c**).

Figure 39c Previewing an FLV in a browser.

#40 Embedding QuickTime Media and Windows Media

QuickTime movies can be easily embedded in Dreamweaver pages, and you can easily reset the size at which QuickTime movies will display. However, Dreamweaver does not provide easy-to-use sets of controllers for QuickTime movies like it does for Flash Video. Features like background color, autoplay, and scale (enlargement of a video by displaying it at a lower resolution) are all defined with parameters that must be entered manually.

To embed a QuickTime movie, choose Insert > Media > Plugin. The all-purpose Select File dialog (which is used for all types of plug-ins, not just QuickTime files) opens. Navigate to the QuickTime (MOV) file you want to insert, and click Choose (Mac) or OK (Windows).

The embedded QuickTime movie appears as a minimalist 32-pixel-square box regardless of the size of the actual movie. To display the movie at an appropriate size, enter a height and width in the Properties inspector. You can also enter vertical (V) or horizontal (H) spacing in the Properties inspector. Use the Align pop-up menu to align the movie on the left or right side of the page (**Figure 40a**).

Figure 40a Defining dimensions, spacing, and alignment for a QuickTime movie.

Useful QuickTime Parameters

Following are a few useful parameters for controlling the display of QuickTime movies:

- The BGCOLOR parameter defines the background color. Enter standard colors (like red, blue, green, or black) or hexadecimal color values.

- The SCALE parameter enlarges a video by making the resolution grainier. Setting the scale value to 2, for example, doubles the size of the video display without affecting the number of pixels.

- The AUTOPLAY parameter can be set to true (the video plays when the page opens) or false.

- The VOLUME parameter defines the default volume for the video when it plays on a scale of 1 (quiet) to 10 (loud).

You have to manually enter display parameters into the Parameters section of the Properties inspector. Click the Parameters button in the Properties inspector to display the Parameters dialog. You can add parameters by clicking the plus button in the dialog. Enter a parameter in the left column, and enter a value in the right column. After you set parameters, click OK to close the Parameters dialog (**Figure 40b**).

Figure 40b Entering parameters for a QuickTime movie.

You can preview your QuickTime movie in the Dreamweaver Document window by clicking the Play button in the Properties inspector. You can preview a QuickTime video using Live view, but you'll have more reliable preview results if you preview the page with the movie in a Web browser (choose File > Preview in Browser, and then select a browser from the available list if you have more than one).

Embedding Windows Media is similar to embedding QuickTime movies except that the parameters are not as standardized or easy to set. To embed a Windows Media movie, choose Insert > Media > Plugin. The Select File dialog (used for all types of plug-ins) opens. Navigate to the Windows Media file you want to insert, and click Choose (Mac) or OK (Windows). A 32-pixel-square box appears regardless of the size of the actual movie. To display the movie at an appropriate size, enter a width and height in the Properties inspector. You can also enter vertical (V) or horizontal (H) spacing in the Properties inspector. Use the Align pop-up menu to align the movie on the left or right side of the page.

Like QuickTime movies, Windows Media files (which can be WMV, AVI, and other file types) can be easily embedded in Dreamweaver. You can also reset the size at which Windows Media movies will display. As with

QuickTime movies, Dreamweaver does not provide easy-to-use sets of controllers for Windows Media movies.

As with QuickTime movies, you need to manually define parameters to control features like autoplay, initial volume, and whether or not a player control displays in the browser with the video.

Here are a few useful parameters for Windows media movies:

- The AUTOSTART parameter with the value set to true plays a movie automatically when the page opens. When the value is set to false, it requires the visitor to start the movie using a control.

- The DISPLAYBACKCOLOR parameter can have the value set to false (no background color) or a color (like red, blue, green, or black), or a hexadecimal value.

- The SHOWAUDIOCONTROLS parameter can have the value set to true (a volume control displays) or false (no control).

There are many versions of Windows Media Player, and they use different parameters. Although QuickTime parameters are standardized and managed by Apple, the world of Windows Media is less defined. You can use Google to search for Windows Media parameters, but you'll have to sort through competing and conflicting sets of parameters. The bottom line is that Windows Media video will display in a visitor's browser window in unpredictable ways. Windows Media is almost universally supported, but developers who need tight control over the display of embedded video turn to Flash Video, RealVideo, or QuickTime.

#41 Embedding Media with HTML5

As noted in the introduction to this chapter, the world of online video (and audio) is rapidly changing and even contentious. Some influential voices are arguing that HTML5—a version of HTML that is being adopted by the major browsers (including for handheld devices)—provides a more open and stable way to present online video. The MP4 video format (and the MP3 audio format) works well with this tag.

As support for HTML5 is still emerging, you probably won't want to make HTML tags the *only* way you present video. But you might use them as an alternative for devices that don't support Flash Video.

Dreamweaver CS5 as of this writing does not have menu support for the new <VIDEO> and <AUDIO> tags in HTML5. So to explore this option, we'll have to resort, just this once, to Split view to look at and enter just a bit of coding.

I find it easy to figure out where to insert code in Split view by entering a title, like "Video," right before I'm going to insert some video code, for example. So, I suggest if you're not fluent in HTML, you enter **Video** in Design view to start this recipe, and then switch to Split view. Locate the text you entered (Video), and place your cursor after it in the code side of Split view. Press Return/Enter to start a new line, and enter code in the Code side.

First type the following:

```
<video width="xxx" height="xxx" controls="controls">
```

where the video width value is the width of your video and the video height value is the height of the video (both in pixels). Use the controls code to display player controls.

Then type this:

```
<source src="xxx.MP4">
```

where xxx.MP4 is the filename for your MP4 format video.

Finally, enter:

```
Your browser does not support the video tag in HTML5 </video>
```

That last line displays text if the viewer's browsing environment does not support HTML5.

When you click the Refresh button, a placeholder appears in Design view (**Figure 41a**).

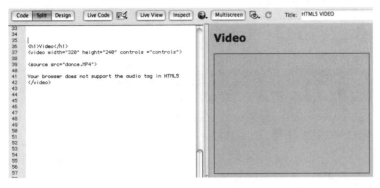

Figure 41a Embedding video with the HTML5 <VIDEO> tag.

The coding for embedding audio with HTML5 tags is similar, and it's simpler. Enter this code, where XXX.MP3 is the name of your MP3 file (**Figure 41b**):

```
<audio src="XXX.MP3" controls="controls">
Your browser does not support the audio tag in HTML5.
</audio>
```

Figure 41b Code for embedding an audio file with the HTML5 <AUDIO> tag.

Previewing Audio and Video with HTML5 Tags

Dreamweaver CS5's Live view does not preview audio and video tags from HTML5 at this point, even with the HTML5 Pack Extensions installed. See Chapter 7 for more exploration of working with HTML5 in Dreamweaver.

Because HTML5 is not universally supported in browsing environments, be sure to preview in the environment you expect your visitors to be using (**Figure 41c**).

Figure 41c Previewing an embedded audio file in a browser with support for HTML5.

CHAPTER SEVEN

Working with HTML5 Pack Extensions in Dreamweaver CS5

Shortly after the release of Dreamweaver CS5 (and the entire new Creative Suite), Adobe came out with the Dreamweaver HTML5 Pack that provides limited, but very useful, new tools for developing HTML5 and its style sheet partner, CSS3. HTML5 is emerging as a browsing environment that, with the support of Apple, Google, and others, allows Web designers to embed video more easily, detect browsers and enable different features for different environments, and easily generate additional effects like rounded corners and transition durations.

In this chapter, I'll show you how to install and use the HTML5 Pack to implement some pretty substantial features it adds to Dreamweaver CS5. Those features are only available in browsing environments that support HTML5 and CSS3, but the list of those environments is already significant, and it's growing. I'll include notes on how to build in alternatives for visitors who do not have HTML5 supported in their browsers.

Arguably the most powerful tool in the HTML5 Pack is the ability to define Media Queries—a feature supported in the HTML5/CSS3 emerging standards. Media Queries identify the medium (browsing environment) of a visitor to a Web page, and present different page designs customized for the particular browser. So, for example, you can create one version of your page for a standard laptop computer or desktop, a second version for an iPad, and a third for an iPhone. This is done by creating alternative style sheets (CSS) for each medium. I'll show you how to use the new Multiscreen Preview in the HTML5 Pack, and walk you through the process of not just previewing how your pages will look in different media but also customizing the look for each browsing environment.

#42 Installing HTML5 Pack

The first step is to install the HTML Pack extension. This is a Dreamweaver extension, and like all Adobe Creative Suite extensions, you can find it by searching the Adobe Dreamweaver Exchange (www.adobe.com/cfusion/exchange/index.cfm?event=productHome &exc=3&loc=en_us). Or, just jump to this URL: http://labs.adobe.com/downloads/html5pack.html.

With the extension downloaded, choose Command > Manage Extensions in Dreamweaver CS5 (this extension only works with CS5). The Adobe Extension Manager CS5 opens. Click Install at the top of the Extension Manager and navigate to the .zxp extension file you just downloaded. Click Select, and the extension will install (**Figure 42a**). You can use the scrollbar on the right to read a description of the extension after you install it.

Figure 42a Installing the HTML5 Pack extension.

#43 Creating New Pages with HTML5 Layouts

The HTML5 Pack includes two new HTML layouts: the HTML5 Three Col Fix Header and the HTML5 Two Col, Fixed Header Right. These layouts are similar to their evolutionary predecessors, the Three Column Fixed, Header and Footer Layout, and the 2 Column Fixed, Right Sidebar, Header and Footer Layouts that ship with Dreamweaver CS5. Despite their truncated names, the HTML5 layouts *do* include footers (**Figure 43a**).

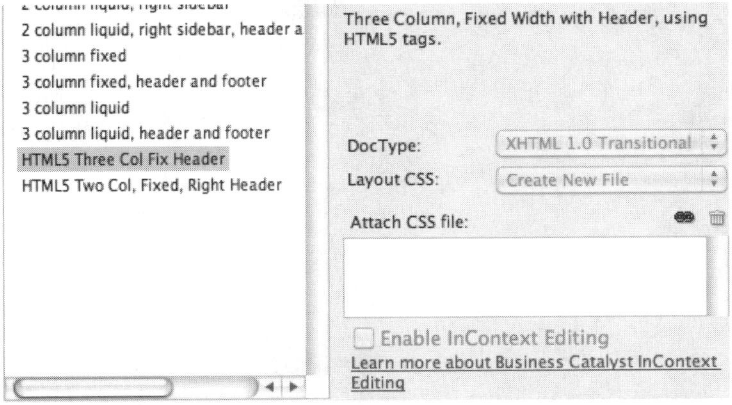

Assigning CSS to HTML5 Elements

One limitation of the HTML5 Pack is that it doesn't update the New CSS Rule dialog's set of elements. HTML5 elements don't show up in the pop-up list of HTML Elements in the Selector Name pop-up of the New CSS Rule dialog. That means you need to type the HTML5 element name (like article or hgroup) in the Selector Name box when you define CSS for an HTML5 element.

Figure 43a Two new HTML5 layouts.

So, when you generate a new page using one of these two new layouts, you won't see anything different in Design view. The differences are in the coding. And, while our book is generally eschewing excursions into code or Code view, it's helpful to be aware of what's under the hood here.

For example, the layouts use the Article element—used to demarcate an independent entry in a blog, newspaper, or other online publication (**Figure 43b**). So, when you edit and clone this section of the layout, you're implementing the Article element, to which you can assign a CSS style.

Figure 43b Examining HTML5 coding in Split view.

What *Is* HTML5?

HTML (Hypertext Markup Language) is the foundational coding that defines Web pages. HTML was standardized in 1999, and innovations in Web design have taken place on top of HTML—using CSS (style sheets) and JavaScript to extend features available on Web sites. Recently, Apple, the Mozilla Foundation, and others developed an expanded and more robust version of HTML. The W3C (World Wide Web Consortium) that governs Web standards has developed HTML along a similar path, and it is expected that the two efforts will merge. That means HTML5 is an *emerging* standard, not supported in all browsing environments.

And the header element (tag) in HTML4 has been renamed the hgroup element in HTML5 (in both cases, the tag/element represents the header for a section); that change is reflected in the code for the HTML5 layouts.

#44 Using Multiscreen Preview

Web designers have always had to aim at a moving target. Unlike print design, which creates layouts that will appear in the same size magazine, newspaper, billboard, and so forth, Web designers have had to guess at the browser, operating system, monitor size, font support, and color veracity. The burgeoning of handheld devices, and Apple's opposition to device-independent development, has multiplied the challenge.

In that light, the Multiscreen Preview feature in the HTML5 Pack is an impressive and quite substantial addition to Dreamweaver CS5. It allows you to preview your open page in three versions: phone (320 pixels wide by 300 pixels high), tablet (768 x 300), and desktop (1108 x 300). To view your open page in all three environments, click the Multiscreen Preview button (which is added to the Document toolbar when you install the HTML5 Pack), or choose Window > Multiscreen Preview (**Figure 44a**).

Closing Multiscreen Preview

Multiscreen Preview opens in its own window, not in the Design view window. Closing the Multiscreen Preview window is a bit inelegant— you have to rely on the close button in the title bar of your operating system.

Finding Viewing Dimensions

Using your favorite search engine, a search for any "monitor size pixels" plus the name of your viewing device will reveal the size of that device's monitor. For example, Apple iPhones have a 320-pixel wide by 480-pixel high display (480 x 320 turned sideways). iPads: 1024 pixels x 768 pixels.

Figure 44a Previewing an open Web page for phone, tablet, and desktop displays.

You can edit the displays of all three of the views in Multiscreen Preview by clicking the Viewport Sizes button at the top of the Multiscreen Preview. The Viewport sizes dialog opens, and you can enter values for other preview sizes.

#45 Enabling Media Queries

Previewing how your Web page will look in various viewing environments is great for alerting you to issues that viewers will encounter looking at your Web page in a pad or tablet. But then what? The solution is Media Queries, a new feature supported in HTML5/CSS3 browsing environments.

In many cases, pages that work fine in desktop mode work fine in tablets as well. The iPad, for example, displays 1024 pixels width, wide enough for most Web pages (which I consistently suggest be designed at 960 pixels wide).

Phones present more of a challenge. Let's walk through an example that you can adjust to solve most display issues for phones. The iPhone display is 480 pixels (with the phone turned sideways). In this set of steps, we'll take the HTML5_twoColFixRtHdr.css file that provides formatting for the HTML5 Two Col, Fixed Header Right layout.

Follow these steps to create a version of that layout that will display well on iPhones:

1. Create a new Web page using the HTML5 Two Col, Fixed Header Right layout. Choose Create New File from the Layout CSS pop-up menu so that a separate (external) CSS (style sheet) file is generated. You'll be working with that external CSS file to customize your page. Save the page.

2. Note in the associated files tab at the top of your open Web page that the associated CSS file is HTML5_twoColFixRtHdr.css. In the associated files tabs list, Control-click (Mac) or right-click (Windows) on the HTML5_twoColFixRtHdr.css file and choose Open as Separate File from the context menu (**Figure 45a**).

Figure 45a Opening a CSS file attached to a Web page.

"Media" Queries Are Not About Audio and Video

Since the word "media" commonly refers to audio and video, the concept of Media Queries might be confusing. The query involved is not what kind of media (Flash, QuickTime, MP4, and so on) is being viewed, but what medium (a cell phone, an iPad, a full-sized computer screen) is being used to view a Web page.

HTML5 Layouts?

For an exploration of how to generate HTML5 layouts with the HTML5 Pack, see #43, "Creating New Pages with HTML5 Layouts," in this chapter.

3. When the HTML5_twoColFixRtHdr.css opens, choose File > Save As, and save the file as **HTML5_twoColFixRtHdr-iPhone.css.**

4. Return to your open HTML page in the open page's tab bar. It's fine to view your open page in Design view. Later you can customize the page with your own content; for now, we'll develop a style sheet based on the template content.

5. Use the Attach Style Sheet (link) icon at the bottom of the CSS Styles panel to attach your *new* style sheet (HTML5_twoColFixRtHdr-iPhone.css) to the page (**Figure 45b**). With the All tab (not the Current tab) selected at the top of the panel, select the original style sheet (HTML5_twoColFixRtHdr.css) in the CSS Styles panel, and click the Unlink Style Sheet icon at the bottom of CSS Styles panel to detach that style sheet. We want to work with just the iPhone version of the page for now.

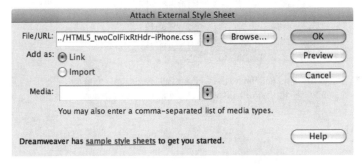

Figure 45b Attaching a style sheet to an open page to customize the iPhone display.

(continued on next page)

Using Another Layout?

If you wish to use the HTML5 Three Col Fix Header layout instead, you can adapt these steps pretty easily to that layout.

6. There are a number of approaches we could take to tweak the style sheet to display properly on an iPhone, without the viewer having to use a horizontal scrollbar. A simple solution (and one you can adapt) is to redefine the widths of all CSS styles to 460 pixels (we'll factor in 20 extra pixels to take into account additional pixels that might be hidden in margins, padding, and other hard-to-detect elements). Change the widths of all the CSS styles that contain widths to 460 pixels: .container; .content; and aside (**Figure 45c**).

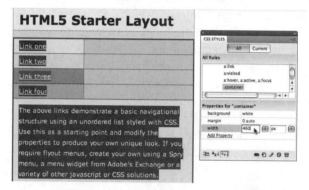

Figure 45c Redefining the widths of all layout styles to fit into a 480-pixel display (with 20 pixels of wiggle room factored in).

7. Now it's time to test the iPhone style sheet in Multiscreen Preview. Click the Multiscreen Preview button, and then in the Multiscreen Preview window, click Viewport Sizes. Change the Phone dimensions to 480 Width and 320 Height (**Figure 45d**). Click OK, and examine your page now with the special iPhone style attached. The page displays without a horizontal scrollbar in the Phone window.

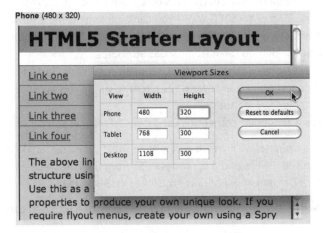

Figure 45d Defining an iPhone preview screen.

8. Next, click the Add Media Queries button to open the Add Media Queries dialog. For the Small (Phone) Target Screen, set Max Width to 480, and use the file navigation icon to navigate to the HTML5_twoColFixRtHdr-iPhone.cssCSS file. For the Medium (Tablet), set Maximum width to 1024 (to match an iPad). For both the Medium and Large (Desktop) target screen sizes, choose the HTML5_twoColFixRtHdr.css style sheet. Click OK to generate Media Query code.

9. A final step before previewing: Change the widths in the Viewport Sizes dialog to 480 for Phone and 1024 for Pad.

10. Examine and test how your page will open in all three environments.

Displaying in Browsers without HTML5

Media Queries should work even if a visitor's browser does not support HTML5. When browsers ("clients") connect with a server, the browser type and version is identified, and Media Queries can apply the appropriate style sheet. That said, there is plenty that can go wrong when you design for multiple environments, and there is no substitute for testing—full-sized pages in Adobe MediaLab and other environments in Device Central, and, in some cases, testing your pages live in the target browsing environment.

#46 Adding CSS3 Attributes with Code Hints

CSS3 Effects

You can easily Google for Web sites that list new effects available in CSS3. One of them is www.css3.com/. These sites provide sample code you can copy into a CSS file in Dreamweaver and then experiment by changing parameter values.

Firefox and Safari: On Parallel Tracks, but Not Unified

As you generate CSS3 code for new features like drop shadows, or variable radius rounded-corner boxes, you'll need to enter two separate CSS rules, one for Firefox (that coding begins –moz), and one for Safari (that coding begins –webkit). Because each of these sets of CSS rules begins with a hyphen, they appear at the beginning of the list of code hints, thus making them easy to find and apply in Dreamweaver CS5 with HTML5 Pack.

Ideally, new CSS3 attributes, like the ability to define the radius of rounded corners or the ability to define durations for effects, would be easy to assign and define in the CSS Styles panel and the CSS Rule Definition dialog. This has been implemented in the HTML5 Pack for Media Queries, which is arguably the most powerful and dynamic innovation in HTML5/CSS3.

Most other innovations in HTML5 and CSS3 are not yet implemented in the same kind of WYSIWG way—you can't implement most new CSS features without resorting to coding. But the HTML5 Pack does provide help with code hinting for those new CSS attributes.

I'll focus on one widely used effect, rounded corners, to illustrate how this works, and point you toward resources to apply this approach to dozens of new CSS3 features.

To create a rounded-corner box Class style, follow these steps:

1. For this exercise, we'll create a new style sheet called css3-styles.css. Choose File > New, and then choose CSS from the Page Type area in the New Document dialog. Save the file as **css3-styles.css**.

2. At the insertion point, begin entering the code for a rounded corner style:

```
.border_rounded-blue {
```

Working with HTML5 Pack Extensions in Dreamweaver CS5

3. Press Return/Enter. As you do, Dreamweaver's Code Hints appear; they include sets of code hints that begin with –moz for Firefox or –webkit for Safari (**Figure 46a**). Scroll down the list of hints until you get to this:
-moz-border-radius

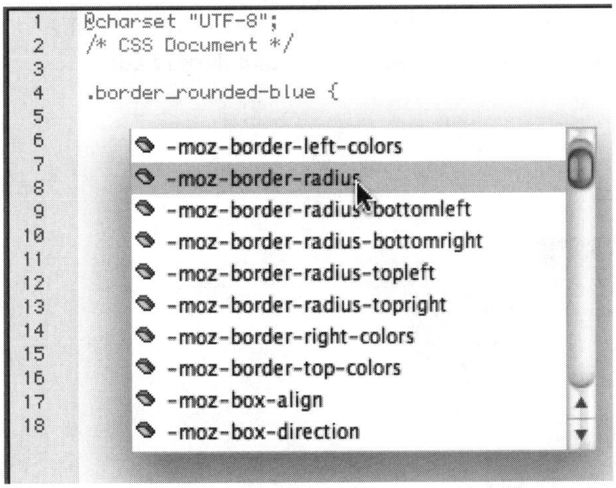

Figure 46a Choosing from CSS3 code hints.

4. Select that code, press Return/Enter, or double-click), and enter
: 5px;

5. Press Return/Enter, and this time scroll down the list of code hints for CSS3 until you get to this:
-Webkit-border-radius

6. Select that code, press Return/Enter, and type
: 5px;

7. Press Return/Enter and type
```
border: 2px solid blue;
padding: 5px;
width: auto;
}
```

You've created a blue, rounded-corner border with a radius of five pixels with the help of CSS3 code hints in the HTML5 Pack.

Customizing Your Rounded-Corner Box

- Instead of the color blue in step 7, type # and choose a color from the Dreamweaver CS5 color palette.

- Experiment with different radii in steps 4 and 5.

- Experiment with different padding and border widths.

- You can enter a value for width, like 240px, instead of using Auto (which constrains the width of the box to the size of the selected content to which the style is applied).

Not all of the attributes in CSS3 styles appear in the CSS Styles panel. Again, this is a shortcoming in the HTML5 Pack. But you can use the CSS Styles panel to edit *some* of the CSS attributes in styles that include CSS3 features. For instance, you can edit the Firefox (but not Safari) radius as well as the border, padding, and width attributes of the rounded-corner style created in the previous steps right in the CSS Styles panel. And you can add other attributes, like background color (**Figure 46b).**

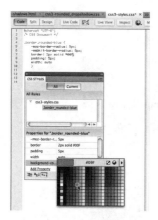

Figure 46b Adding a background color to a rounded-corner box in the CSS Styles panel.

Finally, here's how to apply the new CSS3 style to a Web page:

1. Open the Web page in Dreamweaver, and click the Attach Style Sheet icon at the bottom of the CSS Styles panel to attach the style sheet (in the previous exercise, that would be css3-styles.css).

2. Select an image or text (or any other object, like an embedded video), and choose the rounded-corner Class style from the Class pop-up in the Properties inspector (**Figure 46c**). The effect can be observed in Live view.

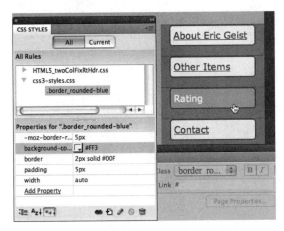

Figure 46c Testing an applied CSS Class style with rounded corners in Live view. The CSS Styles panel displays most of the CSS attributes for the rounded corners.

3. Apply the Class style to as many selected objects as you wish.

CHAPTER EIGHT

Preparing Photos for the Web with Photoshop

Preparing photos for use on the Web and on mobile devices (like cell phones or smart phones) requires saving the image in a file format supported by the browsing environment and then creating the best-looking image you can while keeping the file size low for quick loading on any Internet connection.

Because this section pertains to photos—as opposed to line art, such as a solid-color logo or other image with no photographic or highly detailed content—the two most appropriate formats to use are JPEG or PNG (the third widely supported image format on the Web, GIF, does not present photographs well). JPEG is the standard for photos, and provides the depth of color and detail that photos, even at the lowest resolution, need to look good online or on a mobile device.

So, this chapter will focus on how to use Photoshop CS5 to prepare photos for the Web, exploring approaches and techniques that best handle preserving image quality while generating Web-ready images that download quickly and are accessible in any browsing environment.

#47 Saving Photos for the Web and Mobile Devices

Photoshop's Save for Web & Devices window is almost an application in and of itself. It is the tool through which photos (or other artwork) opened and edited in Photoshop is compressed (reduced in file size) so that it will open quickly in a browser. And it's where you define the type of file and compression to use in generating Web-ready artwork.

Most of this chapter will focus on using the Save for Web & Devices window, and we'll zoom in on some features that make a big difference in how your photos appear online. To begin, let's walk through the basic steps of using the Save for Web & Mobile Devices window.

The first step is to open your image file—in whatever format it was originally captured—in Photoshop. With Photoshop CS5 open, choose File > Open, and, in the Open dialog, navigate to and double-click on an image file to open it in Photoshop.

With the photo open in Photoshop, follow these steps to save it as a Web-ready file:

What's a Good Image Size for the Web?

In considering what size to save a photo to for Web and devices, you need to be flexible. Using a large (up to 800 pixels wide) image can be a beautiful way to present photos. But an image that large takes up a lot of onscreen real estate and takes a long time to download as well. Even an image that will comprise most of the space on a Web page generally should be constrained to about 600 pixels in height or width. And it is almost always a good practice to provide visitors with thumbnails—small, preview-sized images that they can click to open the full-sized image. For instructions on how to create thumbnail images in Photoshop, see #50, "Preparing Thumbnails."

1. Choose File > Save for Web & Devices. The Save for Web & Devices window opens. In the following steps, and in future sections of this chapter, I'll survey options for controlling the quality and size of your image, but one of the great things about this window is that you can choose the 4-Up tab in the upper left and compare different settings. Click in any of the four preview quadrants. As you do, export settings adjust in the dialog (**Figure 47a**).

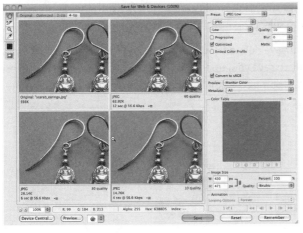

Figure 47a Previewing four options for exporting an image to a Web-ready, compressed JPEG file.

2. As you adjust different settings in the Save for Web & Devices window, you can preview how those settings will look in the selected quadrant of the Preview section.

3. You can increase Blur (the default is 0) to reduce the number of artifacts in your photo. Artifacts are stray pixels of nonmatching colors, common in low-resolution JPEG images, that appear on or near large areas of solid color. The higher the number, the less sharp the image will be, but if you have a lot of artifacts to deal with, that can be an appealing trade-off. The key is to establish a blur setting that reduces the artifacts without reducing too much detail in the image.

(continued on next page)

Window Too Small?

Depending on the size of your artwork, the displays in 4-up mode in the Save for Web & Devices window may be too small to preview how the saved and compressed image will look. If you have the screen space, enlarging the Save for Web window enlarges the quadrant boxes for a more complete look at the image.

Save for Web & Devices Toolbar

The Save for Web & Devices window has its own small toolbar in the upper left. The Hand tool allows you to grab images in the preview windows and move them. The Slice Select tool is used for sliced images (see #58, "Slicing Files for the Web," in Chapter 9, "From Photoshop to the Web"). Zoom in and out with the Zoom tool—hold down the Alt (PC) or Option (Mac) key to zoom *out*. The Eyedropper tool is used in assigning transparency (see #53, "Saving Images with Transparent Backgrounds"). The Slices Visibility tool turns slice mark display on and off.

JPEG Quality for Photos

JPEG is the standard format for online photos. You can use the Preset drop-down list to choose JPEG High, JPEG Low, or JPEG Medium. Higher-quality images look better and download more slowly. For more detailed control over quality, select one of five quality options from the Optimized Compression Quality pop-up menu.

Progressive or Interlacing?

For an explanation and exploration of when and how to assign progressive downloading or interlacing to an image, see #51, "Applying Progressive or Interlaced Downloading."

Color Profiles

Color Profiles are a set of standards for printing and displaying color based on your Photoshop color compensation.

4. Select or deselect the Optimized check box. Selected, the default, creates the smallest-size file possible, without loss of quality, based on all the settings you put in place for the chosen format.

5. If saving to PNG or GIF, use the Matte pop-up menu when assigning transparency (see #53, "Saving Images with Transparent Backgrounds").

6. You might well want to check the "Embed Color Profile includes an ICC Color Profile" check box. More and more browsers can read the profile, so for sites with high-quality artwork, it is worth the slight increase in file size to select this option and attach an sRBG profile.

7. After you have defined your output settings and previewed them, you are ready to save your image for the Web. Click Save, and in the resulting Save Optimized As dialog, choose a location and name for the file and click Save again.

#**48** Cropping for the Web

Often images from a camera are too large to fit onto a Web page. Even $100 digital cameras are capable of taking high-quality images with pixel dimensions in the thousands. Those images must be reduced in size (and correspondingly in file size, to speed up downloading) to work on a Web page.

There are two basic solutions to resizing an image: cropping or rescaling. Cropping cuts out a part of the image, whereas rescaling changes the size of the entire image (while maintaining the same height-to-width ratio so as to avoid distorting the photo).

You can rescale an image in the Save for Web & Devices window. But you must crop an image before you launch the dialog.

To crop an image for the Web:

1. With your image open, click the Crop tool in the toolbox, and draw a box surrounding the portion of your image you wish to retain after cropping.

2. Resize the box, using the handles, as needed (**Figure 48a**). You can also move the box to reposition the cropping area.

Figure 48a Resizing a crop area (the Crop tool is selected in the toolbar).

3. Press Return/Enter. The crop is performed.

Another Way to Crop

You can also use the Rectangular Marquee to select the portion of your image you want to retain, and then use the Image > Crop command.

#49 Scaling for the Web and Devices

The Save for Web & Mobile Devices is designed to fine-tune sizing to match a Web size or Mobile device, not to reduce images from their original (from a camera) size to a Web-appropriate size. So, before resizing an image in Save for Web & Mobile Devices, rescale your image in the regular Photoshop window:

1. Choose Image > Image Size. The Image Size dialog opens.

2. Set Resolution to 72 pixels/inch—standard Web resolution.

3. Leave the Scale Styles check box in the default (checked) state. In the event that you apply a style to a photo (like a drop shadow), this setting will adjust the size of the style proportionally if the image is rescaled.

4. Select the Constrain Proportions check box to maintain the original height-to-width ratio. Also, select the Resample Image check box to allow Photoshop to intelligently handle the resizing process, and figure out which pixels to eliminate with minimal distortion to the image. Generally the Bicubic Sharper options works best for reducing artwork in size for the Web (**Figure 49a**).

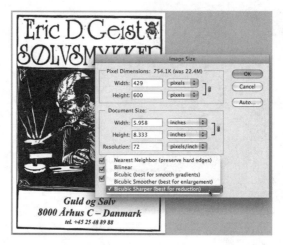

Figure 49a Resizing an image for the Web, and resampling to maximize image quality.

5. Enter either a height *or* a width in the Pixel Dimensions area of the dialog; the other dimension adjusts to maintain the original image proportions. With the new dimensions selected, click OK.

After you have resized your image to something close to the final output size, you can use Save for Web & Mobile Devices to tweak your image size by changing the settings in the Image Size area.

If you are creating Web images that must display well in a mobile device, you can use Adobe Device Central to test your image in a specific device.

To do that, follow these steps:

1. Choose File > Save for Web & Devices.

2. Click the Device Central button to open the Device Central window.

3. In the Scaling panel, choose Use Original Size to see how the image, at its current size, will look in a mobile device.

4. Next, choose a device to preview the image in. Click the Browse link in the upper-right corner of the Device Central window, and scroll down to find the device you wish to resize your image for. Drag that device into the Test Devices panel (**Figure 49b**).

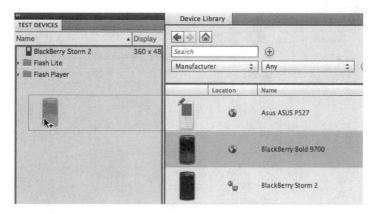

Figure 49b Adding a test device in Device Central.

(continued on next page)

5. Click the Emulate Image to preview your image in the selected device. If the size does not work well, use the Scale To slider in the Scaling panel to preview different dimensions. Note the best display dimensions in the Scaling panel (**Figure 49c**). Device Central will not resize your image; you'll need to do that back in the Save for Web & Devices window.

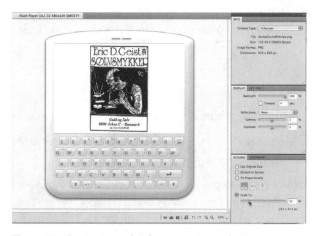

Figure 49c Previewing and scaling an image in a device.

6. Exit Device Central by choosing File > Return to Photoshop. Enter either the height or width you identified in the previous step in the Image Size area of the Save for Web & Devices dialog. Click Save to save a rescaled version of your image for use in the mobile device.

#50 Preparing Thumbnails

One of the most asked questions I get from students, readers, and clients is: What's a quick, easy way to generate thumbnails? It's an informed question—a huge part of the labor involved in preparing images for the Web involves creating small thumbnail "preview" versions of the images that download quickly and take up little page space, but give a visitor a good idea of what he or she will see if they click the thumbnail to open a full-sized image.

Sadly, Photoshop CS5 doesn't incorporate any new tool or feature for generating thumbnails, but here's a tried-and-true set of steps to do that.

To create thumbnails from full-size photos—to serve as links in a thumbnail gallery, for example—follow these steps:

1. With the image open, decide whether you want your thumbnail to show the entire image or a portion of the image.

2. If you want to have the thumbnail show just a portion of the image, use the Crop tool (or the Image > Crop command, in conjunction with the Rectangular Marquee) to crop away all but that part of the image.

3. With the image displayed—in full, or now cropped to the portion you want to turn to a thumbnail—choose Image, Image Size.

4. Reduce the image Pixel Dimensions to the size of the thumbnail you want to create. An average thumbnail size is something in the range of 72–96 pixels wide and/or 72–96 pixels high, but you can enter any value you choose based on the space the thumbnail should be to fit on your Web page.

5. Change the Resample Image method to Bicubic Sharper (best for reduction), so that you don't lose crisp, detailed content in the image when you reduce the image size. Click OK.

Repeat these steps for other images you want to reduce to a thumbnail, or create an Action to automate the process (see sidebar).

Recording a Thumbnail Action

If you are going to be creating a lot of thumbnails (and who isn't?), you can record the steps here as an action, and use it again and again. To begin to record an action, view the Actions panel (Window > Actions), and choose New Action from the panel menu. Enter an action name (like **thumb-96**), and click Record. After you convert one image to a thumbnail using the steps here, choose Stop Recording from the Actions panel menu. To apply the steps, open any image file, and choose the action from the list in the Actions panel; then choose Play from the Actions panel menu. Best of all, you can apply the action to a folder of images at once.

#51 Applying Progressive or Interlaced Downloading

There are two ways an image can download into a browser. Normally (by default) the image downloads line by line. You've probably experienced this. The downside is that it requires a visitor to watch the whole image download before they decide if they feel like waiting to see the image. Progressive or interlaced downloading solves this by having an image "fade in" from blurry and grainy, to full resolution.

Interlacing can be applied to GIF or PNG images in the Save for Web & Devices window. But JPEG is the best format for photos. While JPEG does not support interlacing, you can choose Progressive download in the Save for Web & Devices window (**Figure 51a**).

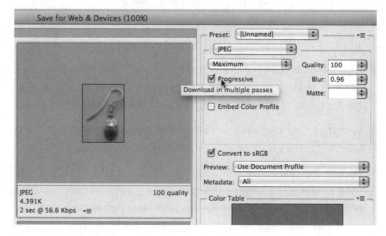

Figure 51a Selecting Progressive downloading for a JPEG image.

#52 Defining Compression, Dithering, and Color Palettes

Throughout the course of this chapter, I've alluded to or noted that there are three Web-friendly image formats to which you can save images: JPEG, PNG, and GIF.

Here's a quick survey of the available settings for different formats:

- GIF, JPEG, and PNG have different compression options. When using the Save for Web & Devices dialog, the format you choose determines which of these options—for compression, dithering, and number of colors—are used to compose the image.

- JPEG offers none of these options, because the format itself supports millions of colors and provides lossy compression, and through your choices in the Quality settings, you determine how much is lost (**Figure 52a**).

Figure 52a Comparing a highly compressed JPEG (right) to a high-quality JPEG (left).

- PNG 8 format offers Dither settings (Diffusion is the default, or you can set a percentage). You can also set the number of colors that will be used to create the image, from 2 to 256. Obviously, the higher the number, the clearer and more detailed the image will be. PNG 24 offers no Colors setting.

(continued on next page)

Lossy?

When images are compressed for the Web, Photoshop calculates how to reduce file size by eliminating unnecessary data. Image formats like JPEG that compress image and file size by reducing data are called "lossy" because you *lose* some of the image data and quality. So, for example, if a photo background is solid blue with just a few pixels of white, compression might reduce file size significantly by eliminating the white pixels.

- GIF, like PNG 8, allows you to choose the number of colors that will be used to compose the image, make a Dither selection (using a definition—again, Diffusion is the default—and establishing a percentage). It also offers a Lossy setting, which allows you to determine how much detail is lost to compression. Another setting offered is Web Snap, which is set to 0% by default but can be increased to force Photoshop to set colors in the image closer to the Web-safe palette.

#53 Saving Images with Transparent Backgrounds

You can save artwork with transparent backgrounds in Photoshop as transparent GIF or PNG images for the Web. Let's break that down a bit: You can create artwork in Photoshop that sits on a Web-page background, allowing the background to show through (**Figure 53a**).

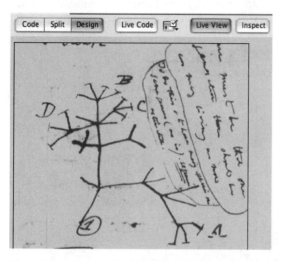

Figure 53a Artwork with a transparent background against a colored page background in Dreamweaver.

Artwork Must Already Have a Transparent Background

To generate images with transparent backgrounds for the Web, the artwork needs to already have a *transparent background* in Photoshop. To make an image background transparent, select the Background Erase tool and use it to delete the background color (the Background Erase tool is in the Eraser tool flyout and can be adjusted in shape, size, and tolerance (sensitivity) in the Options bar. An easier option is to choose transparency in the Save for Web window on a nontransparent image. Do so by selecting a color or colors in the Color Table section of the Save for Web & Devices window and clicking the transparency icon at the bottom of the color table. This works best on areas of solid color. To send images to the Web with a transparent background, choose File > Save for Web & Devices.

Just GIF or PNG

Transparency is supported by GIF and PNG formats only. It is not an option for JPEG images.

Transparency Dithering

When you have areas of transparency within the image, this dithering determines which color to blend them with so that the edges of the transparent areas are smooth and don't appear choppy.

Matte Color

Choose a matte color that is the same as your Web-page background color.

Using the check boxes (and the Transparency Dither settings), you can adjust the display of transparent pixels in the optimized image. There is no dithering option for PNG 24. If you choose Pattern, Noise, or Diffusion Dither (from the drop-down list that defaults to No Transparency Dither), the Amount field activates to the right, and you can enter a value or use the slider to determine how much dither to create (**Figure 53b**).

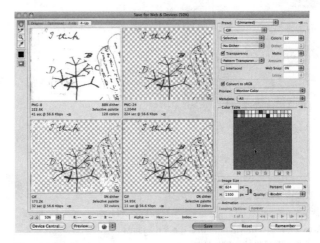

Figure 53b Top left: no transparency; top right, PNG with transparency; bottom left: transparent GIF with no dithering; bottom right: transparent GIF with pattern transparency dithering.

CHAPTER NINE

From Photoshop to the Web

Most graphic designers are most comfortable designing in Photoshop. And Photoshop provides a convenient environment to sketch and prototype Web pages.

The trick is to design in Photoshop in ways that make it easy for you, or someone else, to convert the artwork to Web elements: to design extractable background patterns; to work in design templates that translate easily to Web-page layouts; and to extract artwork or even entire Web pages that can be plopped right into a Web page in Dreamweaver CS5.

In this chapter, you'll learn how to create tiling Web-page backgrounds.

#54 Creating Tiling Background Images

Why Tile?

Tiling background images take up less file size (and download time) than one, much larger image. A 60-pixel-wide background image, tiled 16 times to fill a 960-pixel-wide page, is 1/16 the file size of the larger image. And if an image is tiled both horizontally and vertically, the file size (and therefore download time) advantages are much greater. Tiling background images also provide flexibility—a page background with a single image can work just as well in a 600-pixel-wide page as it does in a 2400-pixel-wide page.

Background Tiling—Simple or Complex

Tiling background images can be as simple as a single, repeating small image. More complex tiling images can be intricate designs created so that they match seamlessly.

Web-page background images are often composed of *tiles*. These repeating tiles match up side by side and/or top to bottom, and repeat the length and width of the Web page.

To create a tiling background image, start by creating a new Photoshop file. Set the size to the size of each tile in your tiled background image. For example, if you want to create a background tile that repeats every 60 pixels horizontally and vertically, create a new Photoshop file 60 pixels wide by 60 pixels tall. Be sure the image resolution is set to 72 ppi. Then follow these steps to create and apply the background tile:

1. Create the tile image. It can be the result of a fill color on the Background layer and then a drawn shape, or a selection from within a photo or other image, added to the image (**Figure 54a**).

Figure 54a Using a small thumbnail as artwork for a tiling background.

2. Save the file as a PSD file for future use—for example, you might want to use the same pattern for another project, but with a different color scheme.

3. Select the entire image—if you have to merge the layers temporarily to do so, choose Layer > Merge Visible (you can undo this or not save after performing this step).

4. Choose Edit > Define Pattern. The Pattern Name dialog appears.

5. Give your new pattern a relevant name, and click OK.

Now you can apply the tile as a background image in Photoshop using the enhanced Fill feature in Photoshop CS5. To test the pattern, and see how it will look as a Web-page background, follow these steps:

1. Create a new file by selecting File > New. Set the size of the new file to the intended size of your Web page, such as 960 pixels wide by 800 pixels high.

2. Create a new layer by choosing New Layer from the Layer panel menu (**Figure 54b**).

Figure 54b Creating a new layer.

3. Choose Edit > Fill, and from the Contents section of the Fill dialog, choose Pattern. Click the Custom Pattern drop-down arrow, and choose the pattern you just created.

(continued on next page)

(continued on next page)

Yes... *That* Fill

Artists who work in Photoshop are abuzz over the new Fill feature in Photoshop CS5. The most dramatic implementation of this tool is to use it to generate replacement fills that duplicate surrounding hair, brick backgrounds, and so on. We'll leave an exploration of those techniques to books dedicated to Photoshop design. But that same Fill feature can be used to easily generate Web-page backgrounds from a pattern design—which is our focus here.

Another Way to Reduce Opacity of a Fill Pattern

You can also reduce the opacity of a background fill pattern by using the steps provided here, and then later reducing the opacity of the layer to which the pattern fill is being applied. Do this by selecting the tiling image layer and choosing Blending Options from the Layers panel menu.

Assigning a Background to a Page

The easiest way to assign a background to a page or pages in a Web site is to define the image as the Background image for the Body tag in a CSS file. For instructions on creating and attaching style sheets to Dreamweaver CS5 Web pages, see #10, "Creating and Linking a Style Sheet," in Chapter 2. You can also assign tiling background images as a property of all kinds of Web-page elements, like div tags, Class tags, or table backgrounds.

Pattern Ideas

Anything can be turned into a pattern. If your tile pattern has a solid background and the pattern is centered within that space, you can create a seamless pattern. Or if the top, bottom, left, and right edges of the tile match up, you can create very complex tiles that repeat seamlessly.

4. To reduce the opacity of the background image pattern, use the Blending section of the Fill dialog to reduce the opacity of the pattern (**Figure 54c**). By doing this, you can preview what your tiled background will look like with reduced opacity.

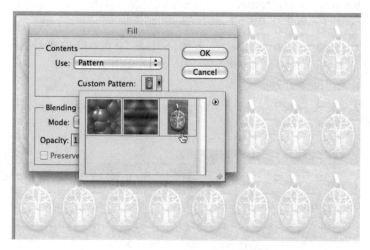

Figure 54c Defining a fill pattern (background shows pattern applied with reduced opacity).

5. The pattern appears, repeated every 60 pixels (assuming you made a 60-x-60-pixel tile). After you've tested (and, if necessary, modified) the background image in Photoshop, save the *original background image* (not the file you have open right now, but the one you completed in the previous set of steps) as a PNG, JPEG, or GIF file (for a full exploration of saving images for the Web, see #47, "Saving Photos for the Web and Mobile Devices," in Chapter 8).

#55 Creating Semitransparent Backgrounds

Semitransparent background fills allow you to assign a background color or pattern to an element of a Web page, like an ID or Class style, but still allow some of the *page* background to show through (**Figure 55a**).

Design Web Pages with ID or Class Styles?

For instructions on how to design Web pages with div tags, see #11, "Creating Page Layouts with ID Styles," or #13, "Designing with Class Styles," both in Chapter 2.

Figure 55a A semitransparent background on a left-side div, over a page with a background image.

The process for creating a semitransparent background is similar to that for creating a regular background image (see #54, "Creating Tiling Background Images").

To create a semitransparent effect for a background or other overlaying image, follow these steps:

1. Create a tiny new file; choose File > New and define it as 2 pixels high by 2 pixels wide. Be sure to select 72 ppi. From the Background Contents pop-up menu, choose Transparent. Click OK.

2. Zoom in using View > Fit on Screen so that you can see what you're doing. Select the Pencil tool from the Brush tool flyout in the Photoshop toolbar. Select a Foreground color in the Toolbar—this will be the semitransparent color.

3. With the Pencil tool, click once to create a dot—just 1 pixel in size—in the upper-left corner.

(continued on next page)

4. Create another dot in the lower-right corner. This produces what looks like a small checkerboard, with four colored blocks. The white squares will later become transparent (**Figure 55b**).

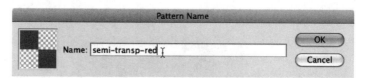

Figure 55b Creating a semitransparent background pattern.

5. Choose Edit > Define Pattern to turn this tiny file into a pattern you can later apply to another image.

6. Start another new file (File > New). This one should be 50 pixels square and again 72 ppi. Again, choose Transparent from the Background Contents pop-up menu, and then click OK.

7. Choose Edit > Fill, and from the Custom Pattern pop-up menu choose the semitransparent pattern you created.

8. Choose File > Save for Web & Devices.

9. Select GIF as the format for this new file, and be sure the Transparency check box is checked. You will see 2 pixels in the color table, even if you have the number of colors set as high as 256—one will be the color you used for your two dots, and the other will be transparent (represented by a white block with a diamond in the middle).

10. Click the Save button and select a location and name for your semi-transparent block.

#56 Setting Up Wireframe Templates

The "960 Grid System" is a technique for wireframing Web sites in a way that makes them easy to translate to Web pages. The number 960 defines the width of the Web page. It's close to the 1024-pixel width of standard smaller-screen browsing environments (like the Apple iPad or many netbook computers). But the secret to the 960 grid is that it's easily divisible into 2, 4, 6, 8, 12, 16, or even 24 columns. Those columns can be duplicated with CSS styles in Dreamweaver CS5 (or any Web-design environment), making it relatively easy to port a prototype of a Web page from Photoshop into a Web page.

The Photoshop template for the 960 grid can be downloaded at http://960.gs.

To create Web-page prototypes with the 960 grid in Photoshop, follow these steps:

1. Open one of the three 960-grid files you've downloaded, and save the file with a new filename, as a PSD file (**Figure 56a**).

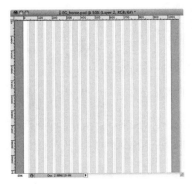

Figure 56a The 960-grid template in Photoshop.

2. Choose View > Lock Guides to protect the layout guides that come with the 960-grid template.

3. Make sure that Snap To is turned on for Guides.

4. Choose View > Snap To, and then make sure View > Snap is selected.

Download the 960-Grid Template

You can design your own Photoshop template for the 960 grid, but that is a bit tedious, and it's unnecessary. Save time by downloading the zip file from http://960.gs that includes templates for Photoshop and other applications. The downloaded grid comes in three sizes: 12 column (960_grid_12_col.psd), 16 column (960_grid_16_col.psd), and 24 column (960_grid_24_col.psd).

The 960 Grid in Other Applications

The 960 grid downloads with templates for Flash, Adobe Fireworks, Illustrator, and InDesign, along with GIMP (a Linux/open source design program) as well as other design applications.

#57 Drawing Wireframes and Mockups

With a 960-grid template set up and saved as a new Photoshop file (see #56, "Setting Up Wireframe Templates"), add content, staying "within the lines" defined by the 960-grid template.

1. If you wish to add a background color or image layer, create a new layer (choose Layer > New, and drag the layer to the bottom of the Layers panel list), choose Edit > Fill, and select your pattern as the fill.

2. Add text and graphic elements to the page layout, sizing and aligning horizontally to conform to the columns in the 360 grid (**Figure 57a**).

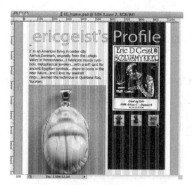

Figure 57a Laying out a Web page in Photoshop using a 16-column 360 grid.

3. After the page prototype is complete, you can save the file as a PSD file, or slice the file into discrete objects and save as an HTML page—as explained in the following two How-Tos.

Ruler Help

You might find it helpful, when designing in a 360 grid, to turn on the ruler in Photoshop (View > Ruler). If the dimensions are not in pixels, Control-click (Mac) or right-click (Windows) on the ruler, and choose Pixels as the unit of measurement.

#58 Slicing Files for the Web

If you prepare a prototype of a Web-page design in Photoshop, you can expedite workflow by slicing the file into discrete artwork objects that can then be embedded in the actual Web page. This saves time and also protects the integrity of the design elements.

Follow these steps to slice a Photoshop document:

1. After designing a Web page with specific elements (like a banner or heading area, images, text, and so on), activate the Slice tool from the Crop tool flyout.

2. Click and drag to create your first slice around a single element in the document (like the banner, for example). A number 1, in blue, appears on that slice, and additional slices are created from the remaining sections of the document.

3. Draw your next slice by clicking and dragging next to the first slice (the common side of the slice will turn blue if literally connected to the first slice), or create a new slice anywhere in your document (**Figure 58a**).

Figure 58a A Photoshop file sliced—the Slice tool is selected.

4. Continue to define slices, using existing slices as your guide.

5. Save the image as a Photoshop file (PSD). In #59, "Saving Photoshop Files as Web Pages," I'll explain how to export all these slices to a Web page that can be edited in Dreamweaver CS5.

No Slivers Between Slices

Watch the slice numbers to be sure you haven't left any slivers between slices—the highest number on any slice (blue for those you made, gray for those made by what's left unsliced) should match the number of total slices you intended to create.

Two Theories on Slicing

One (older) approach to slicing Photoshop files is to simply break them up into equal-sized slices independent of content. This works for prototyping but doesn't allow the content elements (like images) to be extracted from the prototype and used directly in the final Web page. The other approach, modeled here, is to draw slices around specific content that can then be used in a Web page.

#59 Saving Photoshop Files as Web Pages

Once you have sliced a Photoshop Web-page prototype, you can save the entire page as an HTML Web page and the sliced elements as individual images (or text) objects.

Follow these steps to save your PSD file as a Web page:

1. Choose File > Save for Web & Devices to begin saving your individual slices.

2. In the Save for Web & Devices dialog box, note that the Slice Select tool (left-hand panel) is already active.

3. Use the Slice Select tool in the Save for Web & Devices window to select each slice (you can pan or zoom out to see slices that don't fit within the display area) and set the format—JPEG, GIF, PNG—for each one. You'll make your choices based on the content of the slice (**Figure 59a**).

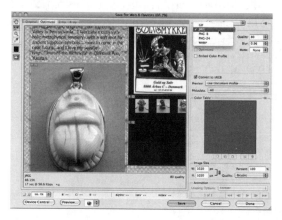

Figure 59a Assigning the JPEG format to a slice.

4. After all your slices have been set up, using the tools on the right side of the Save for Web & Devices dialog box, click the Save button.

5. In the resulting Save Optimized As dialog, enter a filename in the Save As box. Photoshop will add a number (beginning with "_01") to the filenames of the image files produced for each slice.

6. From the Format pop-up, choose HTML and Images to save both your images and to generate an HTML page with your page layout. Choose Images Only to save only the sliced images, and not the HTML page layout. If for some reason you wanted to save the page layout *without* the images, you would choose HTML Only.

7. From the Settings pop-up menu, choose Default Settings option unless you wish to save the page as a single background image (in which case you choose Background Image from the pop-up menu).

8. From the Slices pop-up menu, choose All Slices to save all slices, or Selected Slices to save slices you defined by holding down the Shift key and clicking several slices with the Slice Selection tool in the Save for Web & Devices dialog.

9. Click the Save button in the Save Optimized As dialog to save the slices with the settings you selected.

Ready for Dreamweaver

Each slice is saved as a separate image file, which can then be placed in a Web page. Or if you saved the Photoshop file as an HTML page, you can simply open that page in Dreamweaver CS5 and edit it.

CHAPTER TEN

Creating Artwork for the Web in Illustrator CS5

Adobe Illustrator CS5 is a powerful, versatile program for creating any kind of illustration. Here, we'll focus on a few essential elements of Illustrator that are most useful for creating artwork for Web sites.

Illustrator's power derives from its vector-based nature. As opposed to bitmap or raster-based artwork that is the specialty of Photoshop, vector-based artwork is scalable (which means it can be resized without distortion).

Illustrator is ideal for designing Web banners, icons, and interactive and navigational elements. These elements can be easily copied and pasted to (or opened from within) Flash Professional CS5 or Flash Catalyst CS5, and integrated into animated or interactive Flash projects. Or they can be exported to Web-compatible formats—JPEG, GIF, or PNG.

Far more people are far more comfortable working in Photoshop's raster-based world than sculpting vector paths. We'll address that in two ways: First, I've been teaching Illustrator since before you were born, and I've developed ways to break down how it works. Second, you can create a lot of effective, inviting, provocative, and exciting artwork for the Web in Illustrator even before you get comfortable drawing complex shapes.

#60 Setting Up Web Documents and Artboards

Designing for Multiple Environments

Illustrator allows you to create a multi-artboard workspace, ideal for exporting artwork to many environments. For example, you might use one artboard for a print publication masthead, another for the same artwork resized for the Web, and yet another for a poster. Here, we'll focus on preparing artwork specifically for output to the Web, but we'll note in passing how this fits into designing for multiple media.

Web Color, Raster Effects, and Units

Normally, illustrations destined for digital (including Web) output are created using RGB color mode. RGB mode corresponds to how monitors generate colors by mixing (adding) percentages of red, green, and blue.

(continued on next page)

It is a multienvironment world, and Illustrator CS5 accommodates this by allowing you to choose a display environment when you create a new document.

When the welcome screen appears for Illustrator CS5 or when you choose File > New, you have the choice of creating a document for seven different profiles. Five of these seven profiles are for digital (potentially Web) output. Let's quickly survey them:

- **Web** comes with three (somewhat outdated) size presets, color mode, measurement (pixel) units of measurement, and raster effect resolutions ideal for Web images. It's a good starting point for any project destined for the Web.

- **Mobile and Devices** offers nine preset sizes for mobile device screens and, like the Web profile, appropriate color and other settings for digital output.

- **Video and Film** provides preset sizes and other appropriate settings for various digital video environments.

- **Basic RGB** doesn't offer additional options beyond the Web profile.

- **Basic RGB** and **Flash Catalyst** profiles don't offer additional options beyond the Web profile.

Creating Artwork for the Web in Illustrator CS5

In short, when in doubt, when you're creating artwork for the Web, the Web profile is a good place to start (**Figure 60a**). If you know the size of the artwork you are designing (for example, a 960-pixel-wide, 100-pixel-high banner), you can safely embark on a design project by using the Web profile and redefining the size to match your output.

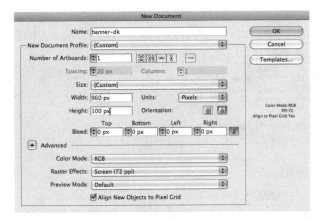

Figure 60a Using Web document settings and customizing output size.

Accompanying Illustrator's massive array of features is an almost overwhelming set of panels. Panels provide access to features ranging from highly useful (Color, Gradient, Stroke, Type) to obscure. As you learn about the techniques in this book, you'll be introduced to the corresponding panels. You can open or close panels by selecting (or deselecting) them from the Window menu. An open panel can be dragged around the screen by its tab, which resembles a file folder tab and displays the name of the panel. Panels can be grouped by dragging the tab of one panel to the top of another panel.

Illustrator's panels generally provide control over existing objects, but you need to use the toolbox to create artwork. I'll introduce you to a good portion of those tools in this and the following chapter. Hover over tools and note tooltips to introduce yourself to the toolbox, and hold your cursor down on those tools with flyouts (indicated by small rectangles in the corner of the tool) to see the entire group of tools. You can select the tool group flyout arrow on the right of the expanded tool group to separate it from the main toolbox, which then shows all hidden tools on that group.

The Advanced section of the New Document dialog also allows you to choose Raster Effects resolution and Preview mode—the default 72 dpi (dots per inch) is a typical resolution of digital viewing devices. The most useful unit of measurement for the Web is pixels.

Documents and Artboards in Illustrator CS5

When you define a size for your document, you also define the size of the Illustrator *artboard*. The artboard defines the printable area of the document. Illustrator documents can have multiple artboards—in effect, you can define multipage documents with varying page sizes within the document. While artboards define the size of printed pages, other document settings (like color mode or resolution, for example) apply across all artboards in a document.

Why Pixel Preview?

One of the great features of Illustrator's vector-based drawing tools is that vector-based illustrations can be scaled to any size without distortion. For example, you can use the same file to print a business card and a bill-board, and the billboard will appear without "jaggies" or dots. That's because Illustrator's lines are defined curves, not collections of dots like images created in programs like Adobe Photoshop. For this reason as well, it is "normally" not necessary to define output resolution for Illustrator curves; they work at any size and any print resolution. If you choose Pixel preview (as opposed to Default preview) in the New Document dialog, you will see images as they will appear in digital output or with the assigned resolution for raster effects. You can toggle Pixel preview on and off in the View menu in Illustrator while working on a document.

One final element you'll want to become comfortable with in the Illustrator environment is the Zoom pop-up in the bar on the bottom of the Illustrator window. Use this to zoom in and out, including to zoom to fit your Artboard on your screen (**Figure 60b**).

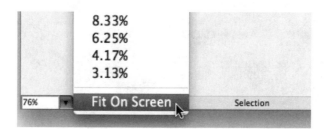

Figure 60b Zooming to fit all the artwork on the screen.

No Space to Draw?

Press the Tab key to toggle between displaying and hiding all open panels. This allows you to easily jump back and forth between all your panels and a blank screen for drawing. Press Shift+Tab to toggle back and forth between hiding all open panels *except* the Control panel and the toolbox.

Guides and Grids

Guides are most easily created by first displaying rulers. To do this, press Command+R (Mac) or Ctrl+R (Windows) or choose View > Show Rulers. Then you can create a guide by dragging your mouse from a horizontal or vertical guide onto the artboard. Although guides are handy, you'll often want to preview your printed artwork without seeing the guides. You can hide the guides by choosing View > Guides > Hide Guides. Guides can be locked, and when they are, you can't move or delete them. To lock guides, choose View > Guides and select Lock Guides. To unlock guides for moving or individual deletion, choose View > Guides and deselect Lock Guides.

Creating Artwork for the Web in Illustrator CS5

#61 Drawing Lines and Shapes

You can create many kinds of Web-design elements with simple lines and shapes. Rounded rectangles make nice clickable buttons, rectangles good banner backgrounds, and a simple ellipse can be a background for an effective logo.

The process for drawing lines and all the available shapes is similar. First, define the fill and stroke colors, stroke width, and other options in the Control panel (choose Window > Control if the Control panel is not visible). Then, you can either select the appropriate tool and click and drag to draw (**Figure 61a**), or you can click the tool once, click on the artboard, and then enter values in the dialog to generate the line or shape (**Figure 61b**).

Constraining Lines and Shapes

To draw symmetrical lines and shapes, hold down the Shift key as you draw. This constrains the arc to increments of 45 degrees. Hold down the Option (Mac) or Alt (Windows) key as you draw to generate an arc using the initial click point as a center point. You can combine both these tricks—as you draw, hold down the Shift key and the Option/Alt key to draw an arc from a center point and constrain the angle.

Constraining an Ellipse

- Press Shift as you draw an ellipse to constrain the dimensions to a circle.

- Press Option/Alt as you draw an ellipse to define the ellipse from a center point.

- Press both Shift and Option/Alt as you draw a circle, using the point on which you originally clicked as its center point.

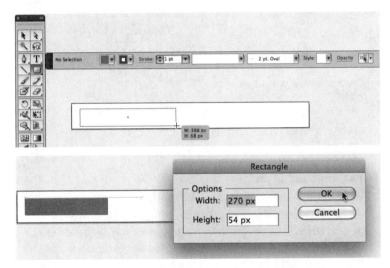

Figure 61a,b Defining a rectangle by drawing (right) or in a dialog (left).

The Spiral tool is part of the Line Segment tool set. The Spiral tool is used to generate multiple shrinking arcs and has additional options that allow you to define the radius of a spiral, the decay (intensity of spiraling), and the number of curved segments.

The Spiral Tool

You can either define a spiral in the Spiral dialog or set the parameters in the dialog and then draw freehand. Since spirals are complex sets of paths, it's often easier to define them in the dialog than it is to wrestle with them on the artboard. The decay rate is the amount by which the radius of each segment decreases or increases from the radius of the previous segment. A decay percentage of 100 gives the appearance of a circle, and anything less than 50 produces something more like a curve than a spiral. A decay angle close to 100 percent creates a very tight spiral. The highest possible setting for a decay value is 150 percent.

Rounded rectangles are a particularly utilitarian shape for Web buttons and elements. Draw a rounded rectangle by selecting the Rounded Rectangle tool from the Rectangle tool flyout. The Up and Down keys on your keyboard can be used to interactively define the rounded rectangle after you click and drag to define the dimensions of the rounded rectangle but before you release your mouse button. Or there is an option in the Rounded Rectangle dialog, which is accessed by selecting the tool and clicking once on the artboard. That allows you to define the size of the corner radius (**Figure 61c**).

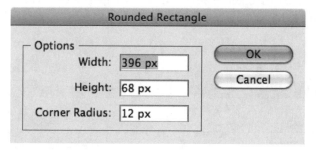

Figure 61c Defining a corner radius of 12 pixels.

Polygons and Stars

Illustrator's polygons and stars can have from 3 to 1,000 points or sides. To define sides or points for a polygon or star, select the tool (both the Polygon and Star tools are accessed from the Rectangle tool gallery) and click on an artboard. Use the dialog that appears to define the number of sides or points you want, and then click OK. When you click OK in the dialog, you generate a star or polygon. When you draw a star or polygon on an artboard, it's as if you are drawing a rectangle that frames the shape you want to create.

#62 Drawing with the Pen Tool

The Pen tool is a flexible drawing instrument. The easiest way to start using the Pen tool is to generate line segments. Note that you generate, not draw. To create a line, you define two anchor points instead of clicking and dragging. You generate a straight line with the Pen tool by clicking once, and then clicking again at another location on an artboard. Additional clicks add more line segments.

Before you draw, use the Control panel to define fill color (if you want one), stroke color, stroke width, a variable width profile if you desire one, and a Brush definition (if you wish to draw with a paintbrush-like effect).

As you generate anchors, the Pen tool remains active until you close the path. If the path is not closed, you add points anywhere in your document simply by clicking. There are two ways to stop defining a line-segment path: Select another tool, or press Command (Mac) or Ctrl (Windows) while you click anywhere on your document to deselect the path. You can change the path by selecting an anchor with the Direct Selection tool and dragging it (**Figure 62a**).

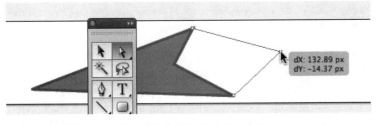

Figure 62a Moving an anchor with the Direct Selection tool.

You can also stop creating a series of line segments by closing the path. To do this, move the Pen cursor over the original anchor point and click (as you move the cursor over the starting anchor point, the cursor displays as a circle).

Once you're comfortable with the process of defining anchors with the Pen tool, the next step is learning to control the smoothness of the anchors. By default, the Pen tool generates sharp-angled, not smooth, anchors. As noted earlier, it is possible to define anchor location and anchor curves all at once. However, this takes some expertise. Start out by drawing sharp corner anchors, and then convert them to smooth anchors. You can do this by following these steps:

Constraining Pen Angles

As with other drawing tools, paths created by the Pen tool can be constrained to angular increments. When you click to create straight anchors, constrain the line segments you draw to 45-degree increments by holding down the Shift key as you click to define new anchors.

Clicking and Drawing with the Pen Tool

There are two elements to the anchors you generate when you click and draw with the Pen tool: the location and the curve quality. Simply clicking defines an anchor point. Once you click—and hold down your mouse button—you can drag your mouse to manipulate the control points to adjust the curvature of the anchor.

Two Ways to Delete Anchor Points

To delete anchor points, choose the Delete Anchor Point tool in the Pen tool flyout, and then click an anchor to remove it. Using the Delete Anchor Point tool removes the point but keeps the line segment intact.

On the other hand, if you select the anchor with the Direct Selection tool and press Delete (or Backspace), this breaks the line segment.

Adding Anchors

You can add anchor points automatically between every anchor point in a selected path. Select the path, and then choose Object > Path > Add Anchor Points. You'll instantly double the number of anchor points, providing more flexibility in manipulating the path.

Smart Guides Help!

Smart Guides provide help in constraining smooth curves; they kick in when control points are moved to angles with increments of 45 degrees.

1. Draw a group of line segments with the Pen tool.

2. Select the Convert Anchor Point tool from the Pen tool flyout in the toolbox.

3. Click an anchor with the Convert Anchor Point tool and drag the anchor in any direction. The anchor does not move. Instead, control points appear. Drag the selected control point away from the anchor and experiment with rotating the control point to control the curve (**Figure 62b**).

Figure 62b Adjusting a curve by rotating a control point with the Convert Anchor Point tool.

Moving control points changes the direction of the anchor curve. Stretching out the control point handles (the lines that connect the control point to the anchor) increases the intensity of curvature. After you are comfortable manipulating anchor control points with the Convert Anchor Point tool, you can combine the process of defining an anchor and manipulating control points. Click to define an anchor with the Pen tool, and then drag to define the control points.

Selecting, moving, and deleting individual anchors is done with the Direct Selection tool. The easiest way to select a handle and activate the control lines is to click an anchor point with the Direct Selection tool. As you hover over an anchor point, the Direct Selection tool cursor displays as an open square.

The Convert Anchor Point tool converts sharp-angled anchors to smooth anchors. It also works the other way. If you want to convert a smooth anchor back to a regularly angled point, click the Convert Anchor Point tool and click on a curved anchor.

To create hybrid anchors, in which one control point is smooth and the other is angled, select a control point with the Direct Selection tool and drag it back into the anchor (**Figure 62c**).

Figure 62c Creating a hybrid anchor with the Direct Selection tool.

Variable width paths, accessed through the Control panel, are new to Illustrator CS5. They allow you to create a line with variable widths. You can custom tune widths with the new Width tools, or choose one of the presets from the Control panel before you draw a line. Or you can apply a width preset to a selected path (**Figure 62d**).

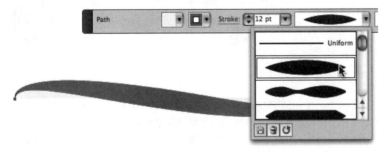

Figure 62d Applying a variable width to a path.

Saving Files

I'll walk you through how to *export* artwork to the Web in #69, "Saving Artwork for the Web and Devices." But if you are saving files to retrieve later, it's easy to do in Illustrator. Choose File > Save. The first time you save a file, the Save As dialog opens. From the Format drop-down menu, you can save files as an Illustrator (AI), EPS, AIT (to create an Illustrator template), PDF, FXG, SVGZ (compressed SVG), or SVG format document.

Cleaning Up Paths

Illustrator has features that allow you to automatically clean up paths. Choose Object > Path > Simplify to open the Simplify dialog and clean up selected curves. The Simplify dialog has a Curve Precision and Angle Threshold slider, as well as check boxes for Straight Lines, Show Original, and Preview. A higher Curve Precision value increases the number of anchors that will be left after simplifying. The Angle Threshold slider can be used to prevent some angle anchors from being smoothed into curves. The Straight Lines check box changes paths to straight lines. Don't be too concerned about the meaning of all the settings in the dialog. Instead, click both the Show Original and Preview check boxes. This will display the original anchors in red and the anchors that result from simplifying in blue. Play with the settings until your preview curve looks the way you want it.

#63 Rotating, Sizing, and Scaling

The Versatile Direct Selection Tool

- Shift-click with the Direct Selection tool to select additional path segments.

- Clicking on an object fill with the Direct Selection tool selects the whole object.

- If you want to select a set of anchors, you can use the Direct Selection tool for that as well—Shift-click on anchors to select them. Or you can use the Lasso tool to select multiple anchors by drawing a marquee around a section of an object or objects.

Group Selection

The Group Selection tool in the Direction Selection tear-off appears as a white arrow with a plus sign. One click with the Group Selection tool selects an object, clicking again selects a group that the original object is part of, clicking a third time selects a larger group that the selected group is part of, and so on.

You can quickly and easily resize, reshape, and rotate any object (or group of objects) using that object's bounding box. If the bounding box is not displayed, you can make it visible by choosing View > Show Bounding Box. With the bounding box turned on, a rectangular frame appears around selected objects, displaying four corner handles and four side handles. You can quickly rescale any selected object by dragging on a bounding-box handle with the Selection tool. Resizing an object with the bounding box expands or contracts the object using the selected handle (**Figure 63a**).

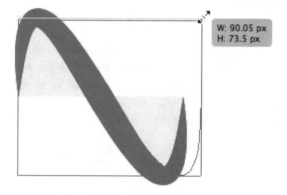

W: 90.05 px
H: 73.5 px

Figure 63a Resizing an object with the bounding box.

Hold down the Shift key as you rescale to maintain the original height-to-width ratio. Hold down the Option/Alt key as you resize using a bounding box to make the center point instead of a bounding-box handle serve as the anchor.

Moving the Selection tool near an anchor in a bounding box turns the Selection tool into a rotation tool (**Figure 63b**).

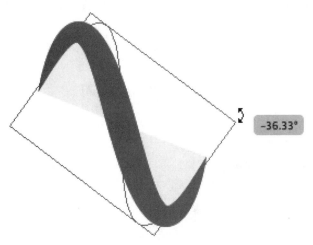

Figure 63b Rotating with the Selection tool.

The Rotate tool rotates objects with more precision and control than you get by simply using the Selection tool. To rotate a selected object precisely using the dialog, double-click the Rotate tool. The Rotate dialog appears. Enter a value in the Angle area of the Rotate dialog to set the degree of rotation. The Copy button in the Rotate dialog allows you to create a second, rotated version of your selected object while leaving the original unchanged. Select the Preview check box to view changes on the artboard as you make them in the dialog before you click OK.

The most powerful and fun application of the Rotate tool is to rotate objects using a selected point as the rotation pivot. To do that:

1. Select the object (or objects) to be rotated.

2. Click the Rotate tool.

(continued on next page)

Select Everything... or Nothing

To quickly select all objects in an open file, press Command+A (Mac) or Ctrl+A (Windows). To quickly deselect everything, press Shift+Command (Mac) or Shift+Ctrl+A (Windows).

Groups

Because Illustrator documents can become overloaded with paths, it is often useful to group objects. Groups can be resized and rotated. You can edit the stroke and fill of groups. For example, if 30 objects are grouped and you change the fill color of the group, the fill color of every object within the group changes. To group objects, select them using the Selection or Lasso tool and choose Object > Group. You can nest groups by combining several groups into another group. To ungroup objects, select the group and choose Object > Ungroup.

Resizing with the Scale Dialog

1. Select the object(s) to be rescaled.

2. Double-click the Scale tool. Enter a value in the Scale area of the dialog to resize both height and width to a uniform percentage. Or enter separate values in the Horizontal and Vertical boxes in the Non-Uniform section of the dialog.

3. Select the Scale Strokes & Effects check box if you want to proportionally resize strokes and effects.

4. If you have an object with a pattern fill, you can select the Objects check box to resize objects. Select the Patterns check box to proportionally resize patterns within a shape. When your object is correctly resized, click OK.

Effects?

For an exploration of Illustrator's effects, see #65, "Applying Effects."

3. Click anywhere on the artboard to define the rotation pivot point, then click and drag on the selected object to rotate it around the defined pivot point (**Figure 63c**).

Figure 63c Rotating with a defined pivot point.

#64 Drawing with Brushes

Brush strokes—applied judiciously—can add unique effects to Web graphics.

Creating your own custom brush is a bit beyond the scope of this book, but a wide array of customizable brushes is available from the Brush Libraries Menu pop-up at the bottom of the Brushes panel (**Figure 64a**).

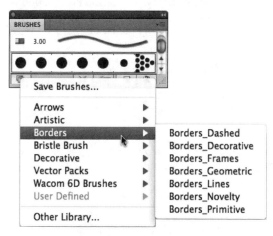

Figure 64a Surveying a Brush library.

After you choose a brush, you can adjust properties like stroke color and width, and variable width, in the Control panel.

There are many ways to draw with brush strokes, but the simplest is to select the Paintbrush tool, choose a brush from the Brushes panel, and then click and draw (**Figure 64b**).

Figure 64b Drawing with a selected brush.

Calligraphic Brushes

Calligraphic brush strokes can vary in size, angle, shape, and randomness (variety) in the brush-stroke width. Stroke shape can range from almost round to very flat, or anything in between. Calligraphic brushes cannot be completely round because they would simply appear as strokes; the "ovalness" of the brush shape is what gives the stroke its calligraphic quality. Several preset calligraphic brushes are available in the Brushes panel.

Art Brushes

Art brushes stretch to the length of any path to which they are applied. One useful and easy technique is to use symbols as art brushes. Open a Symbol library (Window > Symbol Libraries) and choose a library. The Symbol library opens as a panel. Drag a symbol onto the artboard. Then drag the symbol object from the artboard onto the Brushes panel and release your mouse button. The New Brush dialog opens. Choose the New Art Brush option in the dialog and click OK.

Scatter Brushes

Scatter brushes scatter a pattern along a path. To define a scatter brush, start by creating artwork to use as a brush. Small patterns work well. With the artwork selected, drag the artwork onto the Brushes panel. Use the sliders and lists in the dialog to modify the pattern. Drag objects onto the Brushes panel, and choose Scatter Brush in the resulting dialog. Click OK and choose settings in the resulting Scatter Brush Options dialog.

Pattern Brushes

Pattern brushes are the most complicated to modify or create because they involve as many as five different object panels. You can use separate symbols for the start, finish, side (center), inside corner, and outside corner panels.

If you elect to experiment with your own, made-from-scratch brushes, start by clicking the New Brush icon at the bottom of the Brushes panel. Consult the sidebars for tips on particular brush types.

New to Illustrator CS5, Bristle Brushes simulate the effect of an actual paintbrush, with bristles. When you choose Bristle Brush from the dialog launched when you click the New Brush icon, the Bristle Brush Options dialog opens and allows you to define each element of the brush (**Figure 64c**).

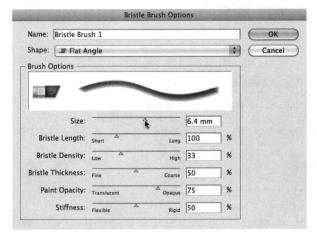

Figure 64c Defining and previewing a Bristle Brush.

#65 Applying Effects

Effects are a way to apply all kinds of changes to a path at once. Effects change the *appearance* of an object *without changing the path*. Apply an effect to selected objects by choosing an effect from the Effect menu and adjusting options in the Effect dialog. Again I'll invoke the word "judicious" in characterizing the appropriate way to apply effects to text and shapes, but with that caution, effects can have a dramatic impact on the look of Web artwork.

To apply Illustrator (mainly vector-based) effects to selected object(s), choose the effect from the Illustrator section of the Effect menu. Illustrator effect dialogs for each effect include a Preview check box, so you can interactively adjust the effect settings and preview the results on the artboard (**Figure 65a**).

Removing or Editing an Effect

To edit or remove an effect from a selected object, view the Appearance panel (Window > Appearance). Effects (but not filters) applied to the selection are listed in the Appearance panel. Double-click on an effect in the Appearance panel to reopen the Effect dialog and edit the effect. To completely remove effects in the list in the Appearance panel, choose Reduce to Basic from the Appearance panel menu.

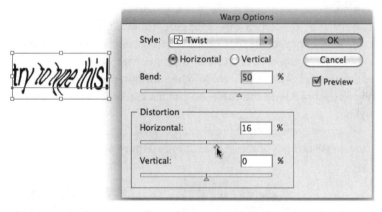

Figure 65a Applying a warp effect and previewing the results on the artboard.

The main groups of Illustrator effects include:

- **3D effects** generate extruded and revolved objects.

- **Convert to Shape effects** convert selected artwork to rectangles, ellipses, or rounded rectangles.

- **Distort and Transform effects** warp, wrinkle, pucker, bloat, and apply other preset changes to selected paths.

- **Path effects** display path attributes (such as stroke) *away* from the actual path.

(continued on next page)

Graphic Styles—Sets of Effects

Because they are sets of *effects,* graphic styles don't affect the *paths* in your artwork; they alter the *appearance* of objects. It's helpful to think of the relationship between a graphic style and the affected artwork as a link. If a graphic style is edited, the object to which it is applied changes. If the graphic style is removed, the object reverts to its previous appearance without the styles.

Previewing and Piling on Styles

You can preview a graphic style by holding down the Control (Mac) or Ctrl (Windows) key as you click on a graphic style. You can add a selected style to an already applied style (instead of replacing that style) by holding down the Option (Mac) or Alt (Windows) key as you select a style from the Graphic Styles panel.

- **Pathfinder effects** apply changes similar to those in the Pathfinder panel.

- **Rasterize effects** create the *appearance* of rasterization without permanently converting a vector object to a raster.

- **Stylize effects** include the widely used drop shadow and arrowhead effects.

- **SVG filters** look like other filters—the difference is that they are based on SVG code used for programming digital graphics for devices like cell phones.

- **Warp effects** apply over a dozen preset waves and warps to selected objects.

More than one effect can be applied to an object. Effects can, in essence, be *grouped* into a graphic style. For example, you can combine arrowheads and a drop shadow or a defined warp, blur, and texturize effect. Graphic styles can include other attributes as well. Stroke and fill colors, stroke style, transparency, and fills can be included in graphic styles.

Illustrator comes with 11 preset graphic style libraries. Access them by choosing Window > Graphic Style Libraries (**Figure 65b**).

 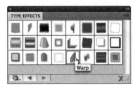

Figure 65b   Applying a graphic style from the Type Effects library.

#66 Creating Background Gradients

Gradients are created by blending two or more colors. The simplest gradient fills involve just two colors and transition from one color to another. Gradient fills can be linear (top to bottom or right to left) or radial (from the inside of an object to the outside).

Gradients can form particularly inviting backgrounds to Web pages and other Web artwork (like backgrounds for banners).

Illustrator comes with several preset gradient fills. To view them in the Swatches panel, click the Show Gradient Swatches icon at the bottom of the Swatches panel. A gradient fill that is selected from the Swatches panel (or another swatch library) displays in the Fill focus swatch in the toolbox. Gradient fills are applied to paths just like solid colors (or pattern fills) are. With a path selected (and the Fill focus selected in the toolbox), click on the gradient in the Swatches panel or in a swatch library.

Let's walk through an example, and you can adjust it with your own settings:

1. Open the Gradient panel by selecting Window > Gradient or by double-clicking the Gradient tool in the toolbox. If the entire dialog is not displayed, choose Show Options from the panel menu.

   Tip
   Expand the Gradient panel if necessary by clicking on the panel title bar.

2. From the Type pop-up menu, choose Linear.

   Tip
   Linear gradients follow a line, whereas radial gradients radiate from (or into) a center point. A linear gradient generally works better as a Web background.

(continued on next page)

Tiling Backgrounds

Generally, Web background images *tile*—that is, they repeat to fill the available space. So, for example, if the content on your Web page is 960 pixels wide and 960 pixels high, you might design a background image that is 1024 pixels wide but only 12 pixels high. The image will tile to fill the height of the page.

Adjusting Gradients Is Now Intuitive!

Gradients are easy and intuitive to fine-tune. You simply move, rotate, or adjust an onscreen slider to tweak the start, end, and progression of a gradient.

Interactive Gradients and Transparency

Illustrator allows you to define the color of a gradient stop (one of the colors that makes up a transparency) interactively: Just select an object with a gradient fill, click the Gradient tool, and then double-click on any of the gradient stops. A small dialog opens, allowing you to change the gradient stop color.

By the way, you can also use this dialog to set distinct transparency settings for different gradient swatches. So, for example, a gradient from yellow to red might fade from an opaque yellow to a semitransparent red.

3. To facilitate assigning colors to gradient stops, view the Color panel (Window > Color) and choose a color mode (like RGB) from the Color panel menu. Then click on the first (left) gradient stop and click on a color in the Color panel (**Figure 66a**).

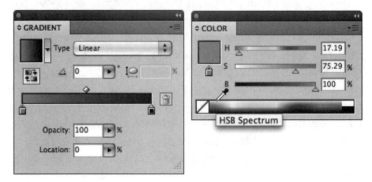

Figure 66a Choosing the first gradient stop color.

4. Click the next gradient stop and select a second color from the Color panel. The fill is previewed in the bar that runs between the two gradient sliders.

5. If you wish, continue to add new colors to existing gradient stops. To create new stops, hold down the Option/Alt key and drag one stop along to the right or left to copy it. To delete a gradient stop, drag it out of the Gradient panel.

Note
You can also add stops just by clicking below the gradient bar where you want them to appear.

6. After you create gradient stops and apply colors to them, you can adjust the gradient fill by changing the location of the diamond-shaped midpoints between each color stop (**Figure 66b**).

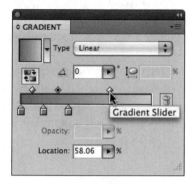

Figure 66b Dragging the slider to adjust the midpoint in a gradient.

To fit your gradient blend to your page background, create a rectangle of the appropriate size (in our case, 960 pixels wide by 12 pixels high). An easy way to do that is to click once on the Rectangle tool with the gradient selected as the fill color, click on the Artboard, and enter the dimensions. The gradient is applied to the rectangle (**Figure 66c**).

Figure 66c Defining an object to use as a tiling gradient background.

Finally, with the rectangle still selected, choose Object > Artboards > Fit to Selected Art. That will resize your artboard to conform to the background image, and make it easier to export the image as a Web background.

Gradient Angles

For both linear and radial gradients, you can rotate the angle of the gradient by changing the value in the Angle box in the Gradient panel.

Saving Gradients

After you create a custom gradient, the defined gradient fill appears in the Fill focus swatch in the toolbox. Drag the gradient into your Swatches panel to save it for future use in your illustration.

#67 Drawing with the Perspective Grid

Using a Perspective Grid for Extrusion

While the potential for three-dimensional drawing has implications far beyond Web artwork in particular, there's some specific relevance, including that perspective grid drawing provides easier access to extruded type (type that appears to be getting bigger as it "comes closer" to you).

Grid Color and Opacity Settings

The Grid Color & Opacity settings just define display, not functionality, so you can leave them as is or tone down the grid opacity by entering a lower value in that box (I dropped the opacity down to 33% to make the grid lines less distracting).

Perhaps the most dramatic new feature of Adobe Illustrator CS5 is the Perspective Grid.

In the next How-To (#68, "Working with Type in the Perspective Grid"), I'll walk you through generating extruded type using the perspective grid. Here, let me introduce you to the basic techniques for setting up a grid. You can define a one-, two-, or three-dimensional grid. Here, we'll focus on a basic two-dimensional grid.

You can apply a standard 2-dimensional perspective grid by choosing View > Perspective Grid > 2 Point Perspective > [2P Normal View]. A perspective grid appears and is active. You can adjust the grid by clicking and dragging with the Perspective Grid tool on the top, bottom, left, and right handles (**Figure 67a**).

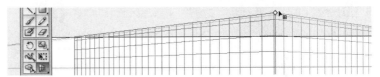

Figure 67a Adjusting a perspective grid with the Perspective Grid tool.

Now, try drawing a rectangle on the perspective grid. On a perspective grid select the left plane in the Active Plane widget (**Figure 67b**).

Figure 67b Selecting the left grid in the Active Plane widget.

Next, select the Rectangle tool, and with your cursor anywhere on the artboard, draw a rectangle. Note that the selected perspective grid is applied as you draw (**Figure 67c**).

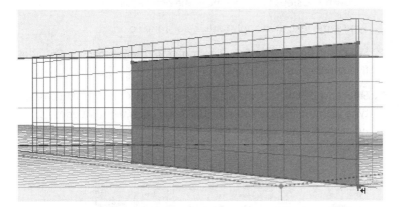

Figure 67c A rectangle placed on the perspective grid.

#68 Working with Type in the Perspective Grid

Use the Perspective Selection Tool for Type

Perspective is not applied to type when you create it; you need to use the Perspective Selection tool to adhere the type to the grid.

Editing Type in Perspective Mode

If you select type that has been moved onto the Perspective Grid with the Selection tool, and resize it with the (regular) Selection tool, the type automatically converts to outlines—that is, it becomes noneditable shapes. The only warning dialog does not allow you to back out of this process; your only recourse is Edit > Undo. As long as you use the Perspective Selection tool (and *not* the Selection tool) to drag type onto a perspective grid, you can edit that type by double-clicking on it.

There is a difference between working with type and working with shapes in a perspective grid: The steps that worked in the previous How-To have to be adjusted if you are working with type.

Follow these steps to place type in the perspective grid:

1. Type some text; then apply fonts, colors, and so on.

2. Select the Perspective Selection tool from the Perspective Grid tool flyout in the toolbar.

3. Select the Left pane in the Active plane widget. Click and drag on your type with the Perspective Selection tool. Align the right edge of the type with the right edge of the left grid, and resize it to fill most of the left grid (**Figure 68a**).

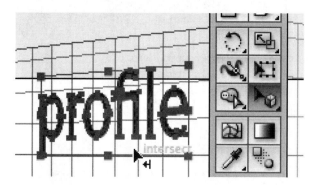

Figure 68a Adding perspective to type as you move and resize it with the Perspective Selection tool.

Perspective Text isolation mode (invoked when you double-click on type on a perspective grid) provides access to Type tools in the Control panel and the Character panel.

CHAPTER ELEVEN

From Illustrator to the Web

You have two basic options for Illustrator files that will be displayed in Web pages. You can save them to a Web-supported vector format, such as Flash's SWF format, or SVG (Scalable Vector Graphics) format. Or you can save to a more widely supported raster format such as GIF, JPEG, or PNG.

If you are saving a file for the Web, all five of the previously mentioned options (SWF, SVG, GIF, JPEG, and PNG) are available from the Save for Web & Devices dialog.

Along the way, particularly when you export your vector artwork to raster formats, you'll have to solve a number of issues: preserving the details in artwork, particularly type, and preventing "jaggies," knocking out the background so artwork can sit on top of page backgrounds, and managing file size, among others.

In this chapter, I'll walk you through the whole process.

#69 Saving Artwork for the Web and Devices

There are three main Web-compatible raster formats. Each has its particular uses:

- **JPEG** is best for online photos.

- **GIF,** while not suitable for photos, works well for images in which the background must be transparent, because it allows the Web-page background to show through behind the illustration.

- **PNG** combines good color support with transparency but is not as widely supported by browsing environments such as JPEG or GIF (as we go to print, a substantial minority of Web browsers are still using Internet Explorer 6, which does not reliably support some features of PNG images).

To save to any Web-compatible format, choose File > Save for Web & Devices to open the Save for Web & Devices dialog. Then choose a format from the Optimized File Format pop-up menu (**Figure 69a**).

Figure 69a Choosing the PNG-24 preset for a Web image.

After choosing one of the preset options for exporting to a Web image, you can tweak the export settings for the particular format you chose. The following options are most essential for configuring Web graphics and are available for JPEG, GIF, and PNG formats:

- **Transparency** (not available for JPEG) assigns a color to "knock out" and make invisible, allowing the Web-page background color or image to show through.

- **Interlacing (for GIF and PNG) or Progressive (for JPEG)** allows images to "fade in" as they download to a browser, reducing the annoyance of waiting for images to appear on a page.

Is SWF Web-Compatible?

JPEG, GIF, and PNG are the three *raster* Web-compatible formats. You can also save Illustrator artwork as *vector* images using the SWF format. See #74, "Exporting Artwork to Flash SWFs," to learn how to do that.

Checking Download Time

The Save for Web & Devices dialog displays download time in the lower-left corner of the window. Download time, of course, depends on a user's connection speed. To change the connection speed by which download time is calculated, Control-click (Mac) or right-click (Windows) on the download time and choose a connection speed from the context menu.

- **Quality** (for JPEG and Curve Quality SWF images) defines how much compression will be applied to reduce file size. Higher quality requires a larger file size. The goal is to get a quality that is acceptable with the smallest possible file size and quickest download speed. You can preview quality on the left side of the Save for Web & Devices dialog. If you choose the 2-Up or 4-Up options from the tabs at the top of the dialog, you can preview and compare file formats and compressions (**Figure 69b**).

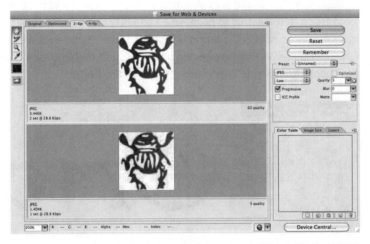

Figure 69b Previewing both a low-quality (bottom) and a high-quality (top) JPEG.

After you've defined Save for Web & Devices settings, click Save, and you'll be prompted for a filename and folder.

Note
If you're exporting type to the Web, see the next How-To, #70, "Anti-Aliasing Type for the Web." If you want to export artwork with a transparent (invisible) background, jump to #71, "Exporting Artwork with Transparent Backgrounds."

#70 Anti-Aliasing Type for the Web

One of the great challenges in creating artwork for the Web is dealing with the low resolution of viewing devices. Desktop and laptop computers—still the way the majority of people view Web content—have pixels per inch (ppi) resolutions of under 100, whereas even home and office printers produce output with resolutions three times that. This poses a particular challenge when creating artwork with type—fonts that look intricate and intriguing in print can degenerate into blurry and ineffective when presented digitally.

Illustrator CS5 introduces the ability to optimize the rasterization (conversion from vectors to pixel-based artwork) of type for the Web or mobile devices with anti-aliasing options that have been added to the Character panel. With type selected and the Character panel open, you can choose from Sharp, Crisp, Strong, or None (**Figure 70a**).

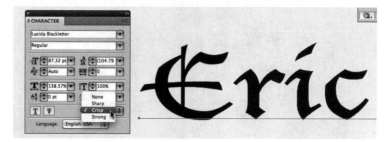

Figure 70a Choosing an Anti-aliasing setting for selected type.

How do you know which setting to use for your selected font? You can preview instantly on the screen, and experiment with all three types of anti-aliasing. For many fonts, the differences are easy to note—particularly if you zoom in (press the Z key, which is one way to select the Zoom tool, and draw a marquee) on your type (**Figure 70b**).

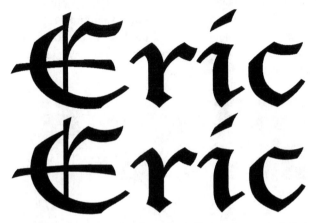

Figure 70b Previewing the effect of anti-aliasing: top—no anti-aliasing; bottom—Strong anti-aliasing.

Saving your artistic type for the Web while maintaining the anti-aliasing you assigned requires a bit of attention in Illustrator CS5. If you choose File > Export, select a Web-compatible raster format from the Format pop-up menu in the Export dialog (PNG or JPEG are supported), and then click Export, by default the Anti-Aliasing pop-up menu in the Options dialog will have Type Optimized (Hinted) selected, thus persevering your anti-aliasing.

Preserving Anti-Aliasing in Type When Saving for Web & Devices

Oddly, when you apply anti-aliasing to type, that effect is not automatically preserved when you export your file using the Save for Web & Devices window (see #69, "Saving Artwork for the Web and Devices," for a full exploration of this feature in Illustrator). To preserve text anti-aliasing when you use Save for Web & Devices, click the Image Size tab in the lower-right corner of the window and choose Type Optimized from the pop-up menu.

#71 Exporting Artwork with Transparent Backgrounds

One option in the Save for Web & Devices window (see #69, "Saving Artwork for the Web and Devices," for an overview) is to create a transparent color. A transparent color "knocks out" the background of artwork while saving for the Web.

To apply transparency in the Save for Web & Devices dialog, use the Transparency check box (available for PNG and GIF formats but not for JPEG). Normally, clicking the Transparency check box (**Figure 71a**) is sufficient for Illustrator to intelligently "guess" the background color and knock it out. The result previews in Save for Web & Devices window with a gray and white checkerboard background.

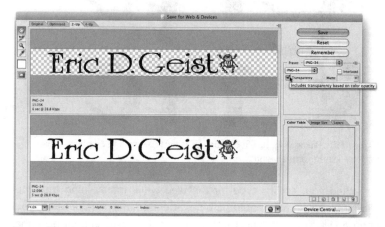

Figure 71a Assigning transparency.

If for some reason Illustrator has difficulty identifying the background color for transparency, click on the Matte pop-up menu and choose either White or Black, and select the Transparency check box. If those options still don't accurately knock out the background, click the Eyedropper tool in the Save for Web & Devices dialog, and click on the background of your image. Then, use the Eyedropper to sample the background color (**Figure 71b**).

Figure 71b Using the Eyedropper tool in the Save for Web & Devices dialog to define a transparent background color.

Troubleshooting

If you are having trouble assigning a transparency color, try this: Since all GIFs and PNGs are indexed (have a color palette), each color shows up in the Color Table tab. Click on one or more of those colors and then click the transparency icon at the bottom of the color table and voilà! The selected colors go transparent.

#72 Exporting Illustrator Files as HTML

Illustrator's Save for Web & Devices feature allows you to save files in Web-friendly JPEG, GIF, SWF, PNG, and other file formats. But not only does the Save for Web & Devices dialog translate your Illustrator illustrations to Web-compatible file formats, it can also save your entire document as an HTML Web page. This page can easily be opened and edited in any HTML page editor, including Adobe Dreamweaver CS4 (or any other environment for editing Web pages).

By default, Illustrator will save *all* objects on your page as a single illustration and then embed that single image file in an HTML Web page when you create an HTML page. If you (or a Web-design associate) will be editing your page in Dreamweaver or another Web-page editor, it is better to first *slice* the illustration. Slices can then be saved as individual Web-compatible images.

To create a slice from a selected object or objects, choose Object > Slice > Make (**Figure 72a**).

Figure 72a Generating a slice from a selected object.

To create a *single* slice that includes more than one object, select the objects and choose Object > Slice > Create from Selection. As you generate slices, Illustrator displays a grid on the page.

When you define slices, grids appear on the artboard. Those gridlines represent table rows and columns that will generate when you save the document as an HTML page (**Figure 72b**).

Figure 72b Slices are displayed on the artboard in Illustrator.

After you create a slice, you can configure it as an image slice or a text slice. Text slices (that were created by selecting text and creating a slice from that text object) export to HTML pages as editable type. To change a selected slice to a text slice, choose Object > Slice > Slice Options. Choose HTML Text from the Slice Type pop-up menu (**Figure 72c**). You can assign attributes like background color and horizontal and vertical alignment in the Slice Options dialog.

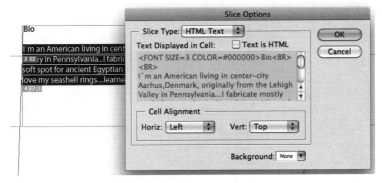

Figure 72c Defining a text slice as HTML text.

Saving Slices in Different Formats

The slices produced by slicing images can be saved in *different* Web-compatible file formats. For instance, one sliced element of an Illustrator file can be saved as a Flash banner, another element can be saved as a JPEG image, and yet another as a transparent GIF image.

Settings for Slices

To assign settings to individual slices, click on each slice in the Save for Web & Devices window and adjust settings. Then when you save, all slices are saved as individual images in an images folder and an html page is created.

#**73** Defining Links in Illustrator

You can use the Slice Options dialog to define links for images (along with other attributes like alternate text and target window). With a slice selected, choose Object > Slice > Slice Options to open the Slice Options dialog.

Enter a name; this will be the name for your image file after you save your entire Illustrator file in the Save for Web & Devices window.

Enter a link target in the URL box, a target browser window in the Target box, a message that displays in the browser status bar in the Message box, and Alt text (alternate text content) in the Alt box (**Figure 73a**).

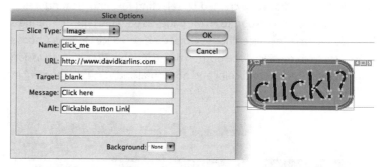

Figure 73a Defining link attributes for a selected slice.

Alt text displays in a viewer's browsing environment when the image cannot display, or is read out loud to vision-impaired visitors with special browsing setups. A link *target* defines whether the link opens in the same browser window (that is the default and requires no additional settings) or a new browser window (the _blank setting).

Slicing?

For an exploration of slicing Illustrator images to prepare them for export to the Web, see #72, "Exporting Illustrator Files as HTML."

Why Assign Links in Illustrator?

Generally, when you create artwork for the Web in Illustrator, you assign attributes like links in Dreamweaver, not Illustrator. But sometimes you do want to define links in Illustrator as you design things like navigation buttons, icons, and logos. This might be useful, for example, if you are creating a wireframe (a rough mockup) of a Web page and want working links.

Saving for HTML

Images (or any object including type) with link attributes can be saved as part of your entire Illustrator file to an HTML file. See #72, "Exporting Illustrator Files as HTML," for instructions on how to do that.

#**74** Exporting Artwork to Flash SWFs

If you want to share files with a Flash developer, simply save them as AI CS5 files. But if you want to save Illustrator artwork *as a Flash (SWF) file right in Illustrator,* you can do that as well.

Flash SWF format is used to play (but not edit) Flash movies. SWF files have the advantage of displaying as scalable vectors online, a property not shared by traditional Web-compatible graphic formats like JPEG, PNG, or GIF.

To save an Illustrator file as a SWF, choose File > Save for Web & Devices. In the Save for Web & Devices dialog, choose SWF from the Optimized File Format pop-up menu.

Use the Flash Player Version pop-up menu to choose which version of the Flash Player to save for. Choosing an older version makes it more likely that the SWF file can be played in browsers and on devices. Choosing the latest version ensures that every feature available is supported when your illustration is rendered on a device or in a browser. Generally speaking, Illustrator artwork can be saved to older versions of the SWF format (like 6, 7, 8, or 9) without losing any quality.

Effects That Fail to Import into Flash CS5

Flash CS5 smoothly accepts Illustrator artwork. You can copy and paste into Flash or open Illustrator files right in Flash. Animators in Flash will be able to edit your artwork, but many effects will lose their "effect" properties and import into Flash simply as vectors. This is because the effects supported in Flash are constrained by what the Flash Player can recognize.

Before You Export to Flash, Read This!

Before diving into *how* to export Illustrator files to Flash format, let's distinguish between two kinds of Flash files. SWF (pronounced *swiff*) files play in the Flash Player and are widely supported in Web and device browsers. They cannot be edited in Flash; they are exported from Flash to play in browsers. If you are exporting Illustrator artwork for use on the Web, SWF files preserve the advantages of vector artwork, including compact file size and scalability. Flash (FLA) files can be edited, but not viewed in browsers.

Frame Rate and Looping

The Frame Rate and Looping settings in the Save for Web & Devices window only apply to Flash animation. See #75, "Generating Layers for Flash Animation."

Higher Curve Quality settings preserve curves with fewer jagged edges but increase file size. The Compressed check box further reduces file size. The Preserve Appearance check box creates limited editability when the file is placed in Flash. The Protect File check box prevents the file from being opened in any application other than the Flash viewer or Flash. The Text As Outlines check box converts text to curves. Use this option for better-quality images (**Figure 74a**).

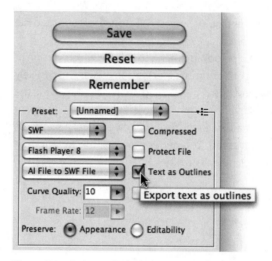

Figure 74a Saving to Flash Player 8 with the highest curve quality and noneditable type.

#75 Generating Layers for Flash Animation

Layers in Illustrator can be used to separate components of your illustration. Because of Flash's vector-based logic, it is much easier to select discrete components of an illustration in Illustrator than in a pixel-based program like Photoshop. And, so, in this highly compressed book of essentials for Web design with CS5 Design Suite, it won't be necessary (or possible) to explore every dimension of using layers in Illustrator.

However, one really cool feature of layers, mostly unrelated to using them as a design technique, is that you can generate Flash animations straight from Illustrator by converting layers to Flash movie frames.

To do that, the more layers the better, so you can use a feature in Illustrator that automatically generates layers from paths. Do this in the Layers panel menu—choose either of the Release to Layers options (**Figure 75a**).

Figure 75a Releasing artwork to sequenced animation.

When you generate layers in the Layers panel, you can either build or sequence layers. Building is better for morphing animation—animated transition between shapes. Sequencing is better for generated tweened (transitional) frames in a Flash animation.

Once you've generated layers, follow these steps to convert the Illustrator layers into frames of a Flash animation:

1. Select File > Save for Web & Devices to open the Save for Web & Devices dialog.

(continued on next page)

2. From the Optimized File Format pop-up menu, choose SWF.

3. From the Type of Export drop-down menu, choose Layers to SWF Frames.

4. Set Curve Quality (as noted earlier, higher Curve Quality values create more accurate curves and increase file size).

5. In the Frame Rate pop-up menu, set a Frame Rate for the animation.

Note
Twelve frames per second is a widely used animation setting.

6. Select the Loop check box to cause the Flash movie to repeat indefinitely. Deselect the check box to play the animation only once.

7. Select the Compressed check box to further reduce file size (**Figure 75b**).

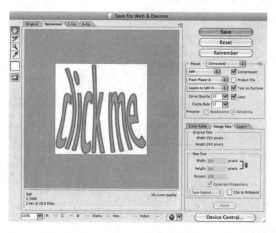

Figure 75b Creating a looping animation from an Illustrator file.

8. Click the Save button in the Save for Web & Devices dialog to export the file as a Flash movie, converting layers to Flash frames.

9. In the Save Optimized As dialog, navigate to the folder with your Web-site media files and enter a filename. Click Save again to save the file as a SWF (with the option of saving a SWF file) in your Web site folder.

CHAPTER TWELVE

Designing Interactive Elements in Flash Catalyst

Flash Catalyst CS5 is an entirely new application introduced with the CS5 Web Premium Suite. Catalyst has something of a split personality: It was created to allow illustrators to prototype interactive elements (like a scroll-bar, a button, or a form), and hand them off to high-level programmers who integrate those elements into complex database-driven applications coded in Flash Builder 4. If you are designing in a large environment with a rigid division of labor and an army of programmers and database geeks, you'll use the techniques in this chapter to hand your work off to them.

Flash Catalyst's native file format is FXP. Those files can be opened in Flash Builder 4, but—and this is a significant limitation for small, medium, and semi-large design environments—Flash Catalyst elements *cannot* be handed off to Flash Professional CS5 developers. But Flash Catalyst CS5 can also create some basic, interactive Flash (SWF) files that can be popped directly into a Dreamweaver CS5 Web site. It is that workflow that I'll focus on in this chapter, even while the techniques are applicable in any environment.

Finding your way around the Catalyst environment will be a breeze. There isn't that much to it. Don't expect to be able to move or resize Catalyst's limited set of panels—they sit on the right side of the screen and stay put. The toolbar is minimalist, with a bare-bones set of tools for selection, drawing, navigation, and zoom. Text editing and formatting options are similarly short-handed. The concept is you will create artwork and type in Illustrator and Photoshop, and then assign interactivity to it in Catalyst. And that's what you'll learn to do in this chapter.

#76 Opening and Editing Artwork from Illustrator or Photoshop

Catalyst's Minimalist Drawing Tools

There's a reason you're being diverted to Illustrator or Photoshop for your artwork. Catalyst has the drawing tools of an iPod App. But it does a super job of importing artwork from Illustrator and Photoshop, and if you have to edit the artwork, it's easy to "round-trip"—that is, edit the artwork in the original application, and then place the edited version back in Catalyst.

Illustrator—A Good Fit

Illustrator's vector-based artwork integrates more smoothly with Flash Catalyst's (and Flash's) vector-based logic. Illustrator artwork tends to scale (resize) better, without distortion, and minimize file size.

Copying and Pasting Works, Too!

You can copy selected artwork from Illustrator and Photoshop into Catalyst, and preserve appearance and/or editability with the same options as if you opened an Illustrator or Photoshop file in Catalyst.

When you launch Flash Catalyst, the opening splash screen prompts you to create a new project from a design file from an Adobe Illustrator (AI) file, Adobe Photoshop (PSD) file, or an FXG file (the native format that Catalyst shares with Adobe Flash Builder 4). Or, if you choose File > New Project from Design File, you can launch a Catalyst project using an existing Illustrator (AI), Photoshop (PSD), or FXG file. And, when you need to edit that artwork, you'll "round-trip" the illustration back to Illustrator or Photoshop, make the edits, and then pop it back into Catalyst.

Let's walk through this. I'll use Illustrator as an example, but the steps are almost identical in Photoshop.

1. Create artwork in Illustrator or Photoshop. A simple, rounded-rectangle button will work well if you want to follow my recipe here. Save the artwork in native Illustrator or Photoshop format.

2. Back in Catalyst, choose File > New Project From Design File. The Import dialog opens. Navigate to your Illustrator or Photoshop file and choose Open.

3. The Import Options dialog appears. Depending on the origin of the file, the options will differ, but the default settings preserve artwork quality while limiting editability in Catalyst. Choose which options work best for you, and click OK.

Designing Interactive Elements in Flash Catalyst

4. The artwork appears on the Catalyst artboard. As I noted in the introduction to this chapter, you'll find only the barest set of editing tools in Catalyst—that's not its job. If you want to edit the artwork, select it (using Catalyst's Selection tool), and choose Modify > Edit In Adobe Illustrator CS5 (or Adobe Photoshop CS5, depending on the origin of the file) (**Figure 76a**).

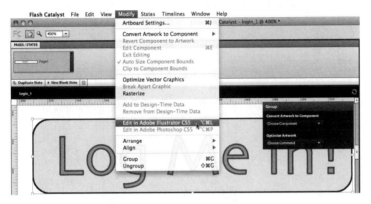

Figure 76a Sending artwork from Catalyst back to Illustrator for editing.

5. When you edit the artwork in Illustrator or Photoshop, a message appears in a bar at the top of the screen indicating that you are editing from Adobe Flash Catalyst. Click the Done link when you are done editing the artwork to return to Catalyst, bringing your edited artwork with you (**Figure 76b**).

Figure 76b Editing Flash Catalyst artwork in Illustrator.

(continued on next page)

Image Quality vs. Editability

When you import artwork from Photoshop or Illustrator into Catalyst, the import options generally provide choices between preserving the greatest (truest) artwork quality, or preserving more editability. If you select the default options (which protect quality but not editability), for example, you will not be able to edit text back in Illustrator or Photoshop when you edit the artwork. You might end up experimenting with different import options to determine which one sufficiently preserves the appearance of the artwork, which is—generally—the bottom line.

One at a Time

Flash Catalyst documents can be more than one page; you can have only one Catalyst project open at any time.

Limits on Support for Effects

When you open an Illustrator or Photoshop file in Flash Catalyst, not all effects are supported. Why not? Because only effects that "play" in the Flash Player will work when viewed in the Flash Player.

6. When you click the Done link, you'll again be prompted to define how your artwork will be exported back into Catalyst—this time with the FXG Options dialog. Again, all the various options essentially offer you a trade-off between preserving editability (of text, effects, and so on) of elements not supported in Catalyst, or preserving the artwork as faithfully as possible and in the process losing some editability in the source application. After you set the conversion settings and click OK, the FXG Save Warnings dialog appears, alerting you to any changes made to your file.

#77 Wireframing in Catalyst

Wireframing is the process of designing a rough, or sometimes a detailed prototype or sketch of a planned Web page. Although Catalyst's drawing features are limited, they do include basic icons and tools needed to sketch out a Web page, into which you can add interactive objects (like forms or buttons) before sending it to a Flash programmer or a Dreamweaver Web designer (which might be you!).

To sketch a prototype of a page in Catalyst, choose File > New Project. In the New Project dialog, enter a name for your project, and enter the dimensions of the Web page you are prototyping in the Width and Height boxes. You can choose a background color from the Color swatch (**Figure 77a**); then click OK to generate a blank document.

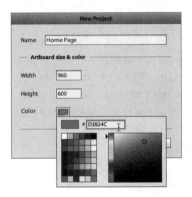

Figure 77a Defining a new document for wireframing.

Use File > Import to add images (PNG, JPEG, or GIF), video (FLV or FV4), sound (MP3), Flash (SWF), another Catalyst file (FXG), or Illustrator or Photoshop artwork to your wireframe.

Use Catalyst's Select tool (or Direct Select, available from the toolbar at the top of the panel) to select or resize objects using the bounding box. Hold down the Shift key as you do to retain height-to-width ratio and to avoid distorting the objects.

Draw shapes with the Shapes tools. Control-click (Mac) or right-click (Windows) on objects to align or arrange them.

What Can You Wireframe?

While Catalyst's drawing tools are limited, you can insert form fields and scrollbars, add formatted text, and draw shapes. This set of wireframe symbols matches Catalyst's set of actions (see #79, "Assigning Actions," for an exploration of actions)—thus allowing a designer to prototype an interactive page that is all set for a coder to bring to life.

Resize Artwork First

Catalyst can only import images up to 2048 x 2048 pixels, so resize large photos and artwork *before* you import them into Catalyst.

Catalyst Wireframes Can Be Interactive

Sure, you can wireframe in any program (Illustrator, Photoshop, a Sharpie on the back of a napkin…). But wireframes created in Catalyst can have some (not complete) interactivity—buttons that change when clicked, links that work, and elements like video play buttons and working scrollbars.

Editing Wireframe Icons and Objects

Use the Select and Transform tools to move, resize, or rotate the placed wireframe objects. Use the Text tool to add last-minute or prototype text, and use the Shapes tools to add simple artwork to the wireframe.

Use Catalyst's Transform tool to rotate selected objects (**Figure 77b**).

Figure 77b Wireframing and rotating an object with the Transform tool.

In addition to placing artwork and media on the artboard, a set of wireframing icons and objects is available in the Wireframe Components tab of the top panel in the panel bar to the right of the artboard. Click and drag to pull any of those components onto your wireframe (**Figure 77c**).

Figure 77c Adding a vertical scrollbar to a wireframe.

To share the wireframe, save it as a SWF file (see #83, "Exporting Catalyst Projects to SWF").

Designing Interactive Elements in Flash Catalyst

#78 Creating a Four-State Button

Four-state buttons—buttons that display differently in normal, hovered, clicked, and active states (or some variation of those)—add interactivity and dynamism to Web pages. Designing a four-state button is easy in Flash Catalyst, as long as you create the artwork in Illustrator or Photoshop first. But wait! Before you expend the energy creating four buttons (one for each state), hit the pause button. You only need *one* button from Photoshop or Illustrator.

If you've got a button ready as an Illustrator or Photoshop file, follow these steps to use effects in Catalyst to generate four "looks" for the button:

1. Create a Catalyst file based on a button you designed and saved as an Illustrator or Photoshop file (see #76, "Opening and Editing Artwork from Illustrator or Photoshop").

2. Double-click on the button artwork from Illustrator (or Photoshop), and assign Button from Catalyst's Convert Artwork to Component pop-up (**Figure 78a**).

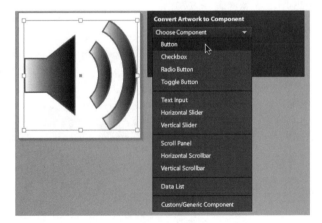

Figure 78a Converting artwork to a button.

3. As soon as you convert the artwork to a button, the Convert Artwork to Component pop-up menu presents four button states (up, over, down, or disabled). Click on any of them to open the selected button state in the artboard (all four button states now display at the top of the screen, and you can switch to any of them by clicking on one).

(continued on next page)

4. You can use the (admittedly limited) set of graphic filters in Catalyst to modify the up, over, down, and disabled states of a button, choosing from Blur, Drop Shadow, Inner Shadow, Bevel, Glow, or Inner Glow effects available from the Filters section of the Properties panel—part of the panel bar to the right of the artboard (**Figure 78b**).

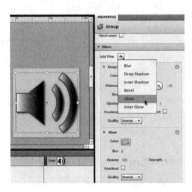

Figure 78b Applying filters to a button state selection.

#79 Assigning Actions

The real power of Flash Catalyst lies in its ability to assign actions to graphic elements. A triangle can become a play button for a video, an icon can become a link, a button can launch an audio file, and so on.

The list of assignable actions is limited to the following:

- Play, pause, or stop video

- Go to a URL

- Play, pause, and stop SWF files, or go to a specific frame

- Change a component's state

- Change or fade opacity

- Add a sound effect

- Move, resize, and rotate objects

- Rotate an object in 3D space

The basic concept in applying actions to objects is that an object with an action attached requires at least two *states,* or pages: the original state, and the state the object inhabits after it goes through whatever changes are defined in the action. For example, a Fade action might start with an opaque object in the first state and end with a transparent object in the second state. The Timeline is used to control the duration of the action, and the Properties panel defines the nature of the action (in the case of a fade, for example, from the opacity level at the start of the action to the opacity level at the end of the action).

I'll walk you through the process of adding a couple of actions to a shape, and you can modify these steps to apply other actions to other objects:

1. Use the Shape tool to draw a rectangle. Give it a solid color fill using the Properties panel. To make the experience more real-life, feel free to add some text and experiment with the limited text formatting options in the Text Properties panel. You can select both the text and the rectangle, and choose Modify > Group to group the text and background.

(continued on next page)

2. Choose State > Duplicate State to create a second state (page) with the same content as the original page. We'll define actions that govern the transition from the first to the second state (**Figure 79a**).

Figure 79a Duplicating a state to prepare to assign actions.

3. Select Page 1 in the Pages/States tab bar.

4. Select an object—the object must be selected for the Add Action button to be active. Click the Add Action (+) symbol at the bottom of the Timeline, and choose Fade (**Figure 79b**).

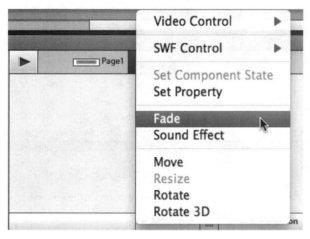

Figure 79b Adding a Fade action.

5. Define the duration of the action by dragging the duration bar to 5 seconds (**Figure 79c**). You can use the slider at the bottom of the Timeline to zoom in and out (to expand or contract the duration spacing).

Figure 79c Assigning a duration to the Fade action.

6. Test the action in Flash Catalyst by clicking the Play button, to the left of the Timeline.

7. Experiment with settings in the Fade Properties panel (like repeat, or adjusting the start and finish opacity settings). Use the Play button to preview the effect settings.

(continued on next page)

Removing Actions

You can remove an action from the Timeline by selecting it and clicking the Delete (trashcan) icon at the bottom of the Timeline.

Using Catalyst to Generate Forms

Catalyst also generates a number of form elements, but I found gaps when I tried to design accessible forms. The set of form fields does not, for example, include pop-up boxes.

Limits on Player Controls

Video player controls are limited to the ability to convert a graphic element to a Start, Stop, or Pause button. There's no option to assign a mute button or volume control. I'll show you how to make the most of these actions in #80, "Creating a Media Player in Catalyst."

Using the Design-Time Data Panel?

The Design-Time Data panel tab on the Timelines/Design-Time Data panel lets you add generic (sample) data to get a feel for what an application will look like when a database programmer connects your interface with real data in Flash Builder. A full exploration of such scenarios is beyond the scope of this book, but here's the short version of how to simulate design-time data: Use the Data List Wireframe component (in the Wireframe Components tab of the top panel on the right side of the screen) to generate bogus data (a list of fruits appears by default). Edit the list in the Design-Time data panel to change the appearance in your prototype.

8. To add a rotation, choose Rotate from the Add Action (+) pop-up. Drag the duration of the Rotate action to match the duration of the Fade action, and preview the combined effect using the Play button (**Figure 79d**).

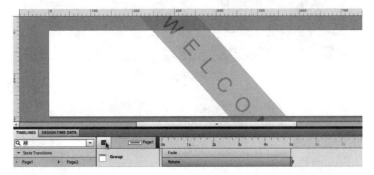

Figure 79d Previewing two effects using the Play button in the Timeline.

#80 Creating a Media Player in Catalyst

You can design custom video player controls in Flash Catalyst, and apply them to an imported Flash Video (FLV) or SWF file.

1. To start out, I'll let you design your own play, pause, and stop buttons. Feel free to do better than mine (**Figure 80a**). If you use more than one object for a button, select both/all objects and choose Modify > Group to convert them into an easy-to-manage group.

Figure 80a Play, pause, and stop buttons to be assigned to a video.

2. Next, you'll need an FLV video. To convert any video to FLV format, consult #100, "Using Media Encoder." Insert the video on the page by choosing File > Import > Video/Sound File. Navigate to an FLV video file, and double-click on the file to insert it on the Artboard. You can choose from three player control options from the Video Controls pop-up in the Video Player properties panel. As we are creating custom player controls, choose None (**Figure 80b**).

Figure 80b Customizing player controls—in this case, turning them off.

3. Now we're ready to convert the artwork to buttons. Double-click on the artwork that will be used for your Play button, and choose Button from the Component pop-up.

(continued on next page)

Keep the Controls Simple

Video controls you create in Flash Catalyst won't be too sophisticated—a play, pause, and stop button are all that are supported.

Formatting Play, Pause, and Stop Buttons?

I won't repeat instructions on how to define four button states here; you can consult #78, "Creating a Four-State Button." But additional options you might want to select for your play, pause, and stop buttons are enabling the Hand Cursor option in the Appearance panel, and entering tooltips like "Click to play video" in the Component panel.

4. Convert the artwork for your pause button, and convert stop buttons to buttons as well.

5. Select the button that will become the Play button, and click the Add Interaction pop-up in the Button panel. From the first pop-up, choose On Click. From the second, choose Play Video. And from the third pop-up, select your video—unless you have two or more videos on your artboard, there will just be one video to choose from (**Figure 80c**).

Figure 80c Defining a button to play a video.

6. In a similar way, define your pause button to pause the video and your stop button to stop the video (**Figure 80d**).

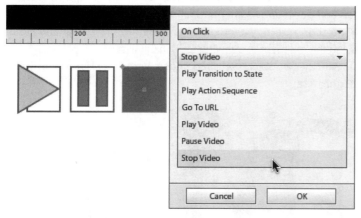

Figure 80d Defining a Stop button.

You can test your player controls by choosing File > Run Project (**Figure 80e**).

Figure 80e Testing custom video controls in a browser.

Video Controls in the Properties Panel

The Video Properties panel allows you to turn on Auto Play, Loop, and Muted (volume off) with check boxes. You can enter Accessible Text for environments that don't support Flash (like "Your environment does not support Flash, sorry"). You can also choose a scaling mode—Letterbox maintains height-to-width ratio of the original video, Stretch distorts the video to fill your box, Zoom expands the video proportionally so if you scale the box vertically but less wide than the original, the sides are cropped off. If you make the box wider proportionally than the original, the top and bottom are cropped off.

#81 Creating a Custom Scrollbar

You can design a custom scrollbar for a Flash application in Catalyst from any piece of artwork. Horizontal and vertical bars work best.

You need two basic elements to create a scrollbar: a thumb and a track (up and down arrows are optional). Create that artwork in Illustrator or Photoshop and copy it into Catalyst, or simply draw a bar and a thumb using the rudimentary drawing tools in Catalyst.

With the two objects selected, choose Vertical (or Horizontal) Scrollbar (**Figure 81a**).

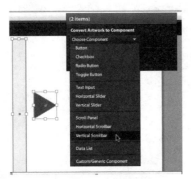

Figure 81a Selecting objects for a vertical scrollbar.

Click Edit Parts to isolate the scrollbar components. Select the artwork that will function as the scrollbar track, and choose Track (required) from the Choose Part pop-up (**Figure 81b**). Select the artwork that will function as the scrollbar thumb, and choose Thumb (required) from the Choose Part pop-up.

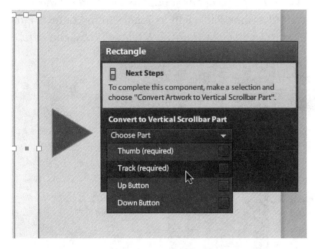

Figure 81b Assigning a part of a scrollbar.

You can test your scrollbar by choosing File > Run Project.

It's a Prototype

The scrollbar you design in Catalyst is only a prototype. It can be applied to a Flash project in Flash Builder, or used to demonstrate or preview a site design with an interactive scrollbar.

Isolation Mode

As in Illustrator, Flash Professional, and Photoshop, you can isolate a graphic element in Flash Catalyst by double-clicking on it. After you edit the object in isolation mode, use the breadcrumb links at the top of the artboard to back out of isolation mode, or just press Esc to back completely out of isolation mode.

#82 Building a Form

Forms, like scrollbars designed in Flash Catalyst, require additional programming to actually work, but you can use them for prototyping Web designs (or, if you're working with a team of programmers, you can turn the form over to them to integrate with a server database).

To create form objects in Catalyst, draw a rectangle and double-click on it. From the Choose Component pop-up, select one of the form elements—Button, Checkbox, Radio Button, Toggle Button, or Text Input (**Figure 82a**). Or, you can drag one from the Wireframe Components tab.

Figure 82a Assigning a Checkbox component to a selected rectangle.

Test your form in a browser by choosing File > Run.

#83 Exporting Catalyst Projects to SWF

When you create a project in Flash Catalyst, you generate coding that is saved as an FXP file—a format supported by Flash Builder 4 but not Flash Professional CS5.

To save your Flash Catalyst project as a SWF file (which is easy to embed in a Web page), choose File > Publish to SWF/AIR.

In the Publish to SWF dialog, use the Browse button to navigate to the folder to which the SWF file will be saved (the file will adopt the name of the Catalyst project).

Use the "Build for accessibility," "Build version for upload to a web server," and "Build version to view offline" options to generate files that can be opened in the widest array of Web environments.

Use the "Build AIR application" to generate a version of your file that will run in a stand-alone environment, without a Web browser.

Use the Embed fonts check box to preserve any text fonts when the project is viewed.

After you define Publish to SWF options, click Publish (**Figure 83a**).

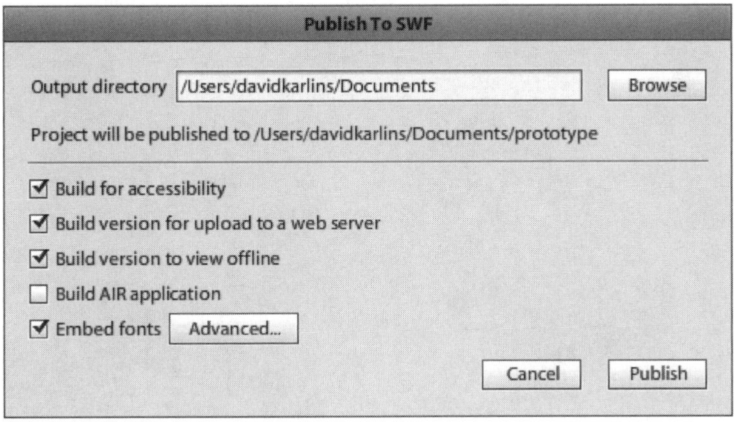

Figure 83a Click Publish once you've defined your Publish to SWF options.

See the Code

To see the coding you generate, choose Code from the Design pop-up in the upper-right corner of Catalyst.

Embedding SWFs in Dreamweaver CS5

Flash Catalyst projects saved to SWF can be easily inserted in a Dreamweaver CS5 Web page (you'll choose Insert > Media > SWF to place them).

Flash Support

Files published to SWF format are currently banned from the iPad/iPhone/iPod-Touch universe. One possible approach, when using these elements, is to make your site nonde-pendent on SWFs. So, for example, if you provide a four-state navigation button, you could also include a text link.

CHAPTER THIRTEEN

Creating Flash Professional Web Elements

Flash Professional CS5 is a powerful application and a "jack-of-all-trades" within the Flash CS5 family. Flash Catalyst is used for prototyping, creating interactive elements to plug into Flash Builder 4 coding, and as we explored in Chapter 12, "Designing Interactive Elements in Flash Catalyst," you can create a number of interactive Flash (SWF) elements directly in Catalyst and plug them into Web sites with no additional coding or enhancements.

In this compressed survey of *essential* Web techniques, we'll focus on two dimensions of Flash Professional: creating scalable (zoomable) artwork and creating animation. (In the next chapter, we'll focus specifically on using Flash to build slideshows.)

Finally, a note on accessibility: As we go to press, powerful forces (i.e., Apple) are pushing to supersede the animation and interactivity that Flash currently provides on the Web with HTML5. First, Flash (SWF) is far from dead—it's supported as widely as any plug-in on the Web, on all major laptop browsers. And there is currently no substitute for Flash Professional for creating dynamic, inviting animation and interactivity. At the same time, forward-thinking Web designers will develop alternate ways to present content (like HTML text instead of Flash graphical type). In Chapter 7, "Working with HTML5 Pack Extensions in Dreamweaver CS5," I introduce you to HTML5, including the Media Query element that detects a visitor's media (laptop, iPad, iPhone, etc.) and adjusts page display accordingly.

#84 Creating and Exporting Flash Files

Flash's native format, the FLA format, is used only to save files that can be opened and edited in Flash Professional (or Flash Builder 4). It is not used to save files that will be viewed (but not edited) on the Web, or in a stand-alone environment. So, you'll save Flash files in *both* FLA (so you can edit them later) *and* export them to SWF (so others can view them on their own or embedded in a Web page). I'll show you how to do both.

Flash Professional CS5 projects can be populated with artwork from Illustrator or Photoshop. You can edit (or even create) artwork in Flash Professional, and—most of all—generate animation. But first you need to define the project.

To create a new project in Flash Professional CS5, follow these steps:

1. Choose File > New from the menu. The General tab of the New Document dialog offers various options for creating a new file. The relevant choice for creating basic animations in Flash CS5 is Action-Script 3.0. Since this ActionScript (coding) is going to be generated by Flash (we're not going to hand-code it), our familiarity with this or the previous version of scripting syntax and features is irrelevant. With ActionScript 3.0 selected, click OK.

2. You can edit the basic properties of the stage in the Properties panel. Choose Window > Properties to display it. Click the Edit button next to the Size area to define the size of the stage—it should match the size of the Flash project you wish to create. Use the FPS (Frames Per Second) link to edit the frame rate of an animation—24 fps is standard. Use the Stage color swatch to choose a background color for the Stage (**Figure 84a**).

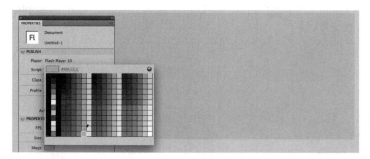

Figure 84a Defining a Stage background color.

XFL Format?

Another option for saving editable Flash Files (besides FLA format) is the XFL format. Saving Flash files to XFL format opens up productive workflow options for complex projects, allowing you to edit embedded images without editing the entire Flash file. Such sophisticated workflow scenarios are beyond the scope of this book.

Why Artwork from Illustrator?

Illustrator is better at creating artwork for Flash than Photoshop because its vector-based environment (that generates scalable curves, not bitmap-based pixel art) meshes with Flash's vector-based, scalable logic. But Photoshop, while not so well suited to drawing, may well be an application you're comfortable with, and for many projects, the artwork copied from Photoshop into Flash is of sufficient quality.

3. When you have defined the Stage, it's a good idea to begin saving your file to FLA format. Choose File > Save. Choose Flash CS5 Document (*.fla) as the Format. Use the Where pop-up menu to navigate to a folder, and click Save.

4. At any point, you can export your project as a playable Flash (SWF) file. To do that, choose File > Export > Export Movie. In the Export Movie dialog, enter a filename (if you wish it to be different than your already named FLA file), use the Where pop-up menu to navigate to a folder, and leave the Format set to SWF Movie. Click Save.

You can preview an animation at any time by choosing Control > Test Movie > in Flash Professional. The animation will play in the Flash Player.

Export to QuickTime, Animated GIF, Sequences

Other export options (besides SWF) allow you to export a Flash animation as a QuickTime movie or an animated GIF file, or to sequence all the frames in your animation to image files.

Other File Type Options?

Additional file type options in the General Tab of the New Document dialog provide a head start if you are designing for specialized environments like AIR (stand-alone Flash applications that do not require the Flash Player) or mobile devices. However, you can export any project to these platforms during the saving and exporting process.

Templates

Feel free to explore the Templates tab. The Advertising category provides a set of helpful stage (viewable workspace) sizes. Other categories open preset animations with artwork. We'll explore the most widely applicable of these templates, the ones that generate slideshows, in Chapter 14, "Creating Slideshows in Flash Professional."

#85 Drawing in Flash CS5

Can we cover drawing strokes and fills in Flash Professional CS5 in a few pages in this highly compressed book? A bit. I'll show you how to define and draw strokes and fills so that you can create basic artwork for Flash projects, but I'll advise you to create your artwork in Illustrator (or Photoshop) and import it into Flash since that works so seamlessly.

The Flash Tools panel includes several tools for quickly drawing shapes. The Rectangle tool, for example, draws rectangles with square or rounded corners, and the Oval tool draws ovals (including circles). The easiest way to define shape parameters is to select them in the Properties panel before you draw. The Rectangle tool Properties panel, for example, allows you to define Stroke and Fill colors, Stroke (width), (Stroke) Style, Caps and Joins (how strokes end or meet), and rounded rectangle radii (**Figure 85a**).

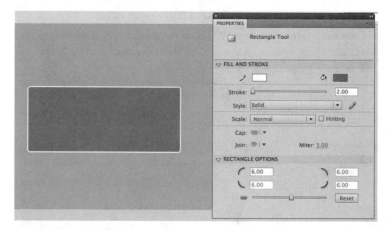

Figure 85a Defining and drawing a rectangle with a white, 2-pixel-wide stroke, a brown fill, and rounded corners.

You can click once on a stroke to select the segment of the stroke you clicked, or double-click to select the entire continuous stroke (**Figure 85b**).

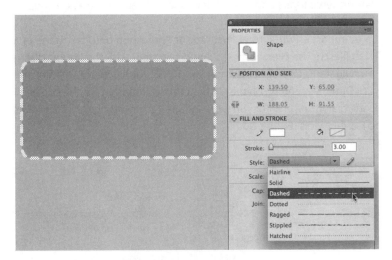

Figure 85b Editing properties of a selected stroke.

To select *both* a shape's stroke and fill (before moving or resizing), double-click on the fill (**Figure 85c**).

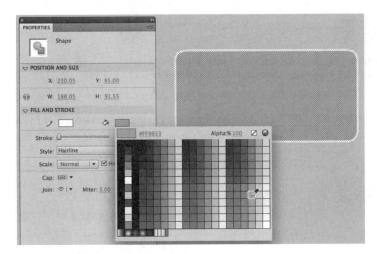

Figure 85c Editing a selected entire shape.

#86 Importing Artwork from Illustrator or Photoshop

Not All Filters and Effects Are Preserved!

Not all Illustrator effects or Photoshop filters can be supported *as effects and filters* in Flash. The limitation is the capacity of the Flash Player to generate those effects and filters. More recent versions of Flash Player support more effects and filters. Effects and filters that cannot be imported are converted to regular artwork.

The best way to create artwork in Flash CS5 is to create it not in Flash but in Illustrator or Photoshop. Flash CS5 has powerful import features that preserve layers and many filters or effects applied in Photoshop or Illustrator.

To import artwork from Illustrator or Photoshop onto the Stage of a Flash file, choose File > Import > Import to Stage. Use the Import dialog to navigate to and select a Photoshop (PSD) or Illustrator (AI) file, and click Open. Depending on the elements in the imported file, the Import to Stage dialog will prompt you with options for converting those elements to Flash objects (**Figure 86a**).

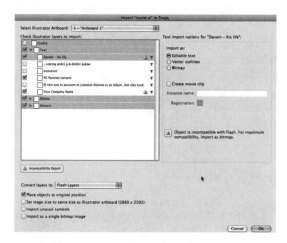

Figure 86a Options for importing an Illustrator file onto the Flash CS5 Stage—here choosing to import selected type as editable text.

After you examine and choose import options for elements that must be converted to Flash objects, click OK to import the artwork onto the Flash Stage.

#87 Using the Text Layout Framework (TLF)

The single most dramatic change in the design capacity of Flash Professional in CS5 may well be the addition of near-print-level typography tools. The new Text Layout Framework (TLF) elevates Flash's text formatting options substantially. TLF can apply column formatting, including column threading so designers can flow type between columns as they would in Illustrator or InDesign. Another intriguing development is the ability to define leading (vertical line spacing) and kerning (horizontal spacing between characters).

To create text using TLF features, click the Text tool and view the Properties panel (Window > Properties if it is not visible). From the Text Engine (top) pop-up menu, choose TLF to take advantage of new TLF format features. From the Text Type pop-up menu (below the Text Engine pop-up menu), choose from the options Read Only, Selectable (text that can be copied and pasted through the clipboard), or Editable (viewers can change the text in the Flash Player).

Font formatting is controlled in the Character settings section of the Properties panel. In addition to font Family (like Verdana or Courier), Size, and color, you can define vertical spacing between lines of type as well as kerning (spacing between characters) (**Figure 87a**).

Vertical Type... and Underlining!

With TLF, Flash can work with editable type that flows vertically (mainly used for Asian languages). And with CS5, Flash finally allows underlining text.

Kerning in Flash

The only option for Kerning in Flash CS5 is auto-kerning on or off. In Illustrator kerning is done differently. There, besides auto-kerning, to kern you just place your cursor between two characters and don't select the characters.

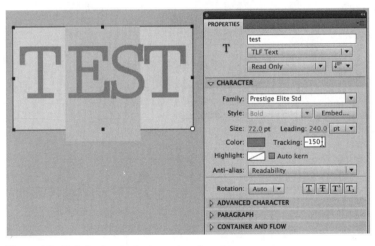

Figure 87a Defining kerning between two characters.

Defining Links

Looking for an easy way to assign hyperlinks to text? You can do that in the Advanced Character section of the Text Properties panel. Just keep in mind that you cannot assign links to editable text in the Text Properties panel.

Editable Text?

Providing editable text can give visitors to a Web site an interesting interactive engagement, such as "Type YOUR NAME here." You cannot assign links to editable text in the Text Properties panel, but you might use this in some interactive application, like a game.

The Advanced Character section provides a high level of typographic control for features like links and link targets (what browser window a link opens in). The Paragraph section of the Text Properties panel defines position (left, right, middle, or full, with various options for that).

The Container and Flow section of the panel defines the box around text as well as column flow. The Color Effect sections enables effects like tint and brightness. The Display section allows you to define different kinds of opacity/transparency.

#**88** Creating a Timeline

Let's create a simple interactive Flash element to add a bit of tension and drama to a Web-page banner. In this How-To, we'll do the first part of the project—create a timeline with two different frames and different content in each frame.

In the following How-To, we'll add ActionScripting (don't worry, no coding required) so that the two frames become a two-frame interactive Flash object, where visitors click to reveal the contents of the second frame.

In this case, I'll use the example of a banner, but you can adjust the How-To for any kind of interactive Flash object that can be plopped anywhere on a Web page:

1. Create a new Flash file by choosing File > New; make sure ActionScript 3.0 is selected in the Type column, and click OK.

2. Size the Stage to fit a Web-page banner. With nothing selected, the Properties panel defines the Stage and other file properties. Click the Edit button in the Properties section of the Properties panel (sounds redundant, I know), and enter dimensions: 960 px wide, 100 px high (**Figure 88a**). You can redefine the Stage background color here as well using the Background Color swatch. Then click OK.

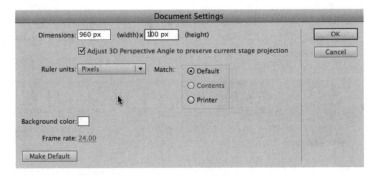

Figure 88a Redefining the artboard size for a banner.

3. Choose Window > Timeline to view the Timeline on the bottom of the Stage, if it is not visible. The Timeline is where both interactivity and animation are managed (see sidebars). Here, we'll use the Timeline to create content in two different *frames*.

(continued on next page)

Inserting Flash in Web Pages

For a full exploration of how to embed Flash movies (SWFs) in Web pages, see #38, "Embedding Flash (SWF)," in Chapter 6.

Adjusting 3D Perspective Angle

When you define (or change) the artboard size in Flash CS5, you are prompted with a check box that says "Adjust 3d perspective angle to preserve current stage projection." This allows the artboard to adjust to fit 3D animation—a feature beyond the scope of this quick survey of Flash. But there's no harm in leaving the check box in the default, checked state.

Managing Type?

For a compressed survey of how to create and edit type in Flash CS5, see #87, "Using the Text Layout Framework (TLF)."

Timeline Frames

The Timeline grid is composed of layers and frames. Frames can be thought of as similar to frames in a movie. When used to manage animation, they display iterations of artwork that, when played in sequence, look animated. When used to manage interactivity—as we are doing here—they control what is displayed in response to actions by a viewer.

Timeline Layers

Flash objects (also called Flash movies) can have more than one dimension of frames. For example, an animation background, in one layer, might be static, while the artwork in the foreground (a second layer) is animated. In addition, actions—snippets of coding that control interactivity—have their own layer. Flash CS5 is cool enough to generally generate new layers as needed for actions, and even for animation when needed.

4. By default, any artwork you create will be in the first frame. Select the Text tool, and enter and format small type (something like 14 points) that says "Click here to see our new logo" (**Figure 88b**).

Figure 88b Entering text in the first frame of a Flash object.

5. Next click in the second frame in the Timeline, and choose Insert > Timeline > Blank Keyframe to create a second, clear frame on the Timeline.

6. In the second frame, enter text and/or paste artwork from Illustrator or Photoshop (or create artwork in Flash) for a banner or logo (**Figure 88c**).

Figure 88c Adding content to the second frame (a blank keyframe) in a Flash movie.

Now that we've constructed a two-frame Flash project, we're ready to add interactive coding with Code Snippets. I'll show you how to do that in the next How-To.

#89 Using Code Snippets

Here, we'll pick up where we left off in #88, "Creating a Timeline." That How-To left us with distinct content in frame 1 and frame 2 of a Flash Timeline. Now, we'll add actions (scripting) that make the project interactive, so that clicking (on content in the first frame) displays new content (the second frame).

Follow these steps to generate coding using to move from frame 1 to frame 2.

1. Choose Window > Code Snippets to open the Code Snippets panel (if it is not open).

2. Click in the Timeline on the first frame. We're going to generate some code to stop the movie here when the Flash object opens in a Web page, rather than have it simply display both frames in sequence. With the first frame selected, expand the Timeline Navigation section of the Code Snippets, and double-click on Stop at this Frame (**Figure 89a**). Two things happen: Flash adds an Actions layer to the Timeline, and an ActionScript 3 code snippet (script) is generated and displayed in the Actions panel.

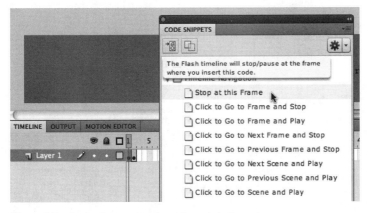

Figure 89a Generating a code snippet to apply to frame 1.

(continued on next page)

Timeline Snippets

With the enhancement of Code Snippets in Flash Professional CS5, Timeline navigation is now more accessible: The Timeline Navigation section of Code Snippets allows a designer to stop a movie at a set frame, to go to another frame and stop, to play a movie, or to go to a defined scene within a movie and play it.

More Snippets

Interactivity, up to and including the ability to generate games, is available from Code Snippets in the Animation list.

Code Snippets and the Actions Panel

When you generate a code snippet, the coding appears in the Actions panel with helpful documentation on how to tweak or adjust the animation or interactivity. That makes the code snippets editable even if you don't know Flash's Action-Script 3 coding language.

3. Next, use the Selection tool to select text that will activate an action to display the contents of the second frame. With that text selected, back in the Code Snippets panel, double-click on Click to Go to Next Frame and Stop (**Figure 89b**). A warning dialog appears telling you that Flash is creating a symbol instance to make the generated code work—that's fine. Click OK in that dialog. Again, the Actions panel opens displaying the new generated code.

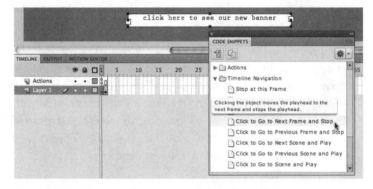

Figure 89b Adding ActionScript to go to the next frame of the movie and stop.

Test your movie by choosing Control > Test Movie > in Flash Professional.

Embedding Fonts

You must either choose Text > Font Embedding from the main menu or, with the Text tool selected, in the Characters section of the Properties panel choose the font and click Embed to open the Font Embedding panel. On the ActionScript tab you must click Export for ActionScript before you are allowed to choose TLF. Complex, but it works.

#90 Creating an Animated Movie

Flash is about interactivity (see #89, "Using Code Snippets" for an example) and animation. The metaphor of flipping through a set of drawings to simulate animation is helpful to understand how Flash works, but Flash CS5 actually *generates* the "in-between" artwork needed to make animation work.

Follow the steps to make artwork on a banner move. I'll assume:

- You have a new Flash file open, with the artboard defined in size and color.

- Your Flash movie has just one frame, with the artwork in it.

With that in place, here we go:

1. With the artwork selected, choose Insert > Motion Tween. A warning dialog will prompt you to convert the artwork to a symbol so it can be animated—click OK in that dialog. Twenty-four frames will be generated on the Timeline—one second of animation using the standard frame rate of fps (**Figure 90a**).

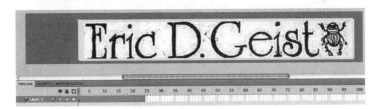

Figure 90a A generated motion tween with 24 frames.

2. Click on the 24th frame, and choose Insert > Keyframe. Keyframes anchor animation start and end points.

(continued on next page)

Global Concepts

While the animation in this How-To is simple, it incorporates all the basic elements of more complex animations: applying a motion tween to artwork (and letting Flash automatically convert that artwork to a programmable symbol), defining multiple keyframes to control the motion path, and adding a Stop action at the end of the animation (unless you want it to loop).

Classic Tweens?

Classic tweens are basically the same as generated motion tweens except that they require more knowledge of Flash and working with the Timeline. Motion tweens in Flash CS5 automate most of the steps required to generate animation. There are some animated effects that require the additional steps in classic tweens.

3. Click again on the first frame, and move the artwork. A line appears, tracing the motion of the animation. You can drag the scrubber head on the Timeline to preview the animation (**Figure 90b**).

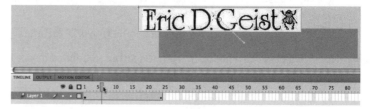

Figure 90b Previewing a defined motion tween.

4. To make the animation more interesting, add another keyframe in the 12th frame. With that new keyframe selected, move the artwork again to create a more complex animation path (**Figure 90c**).

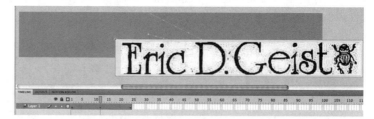

Figure 90c Adding an additional keyframe and adjusting an animation path.

5. To slow the animation, click on a section of the artboard that does not have any content, and view the Properties panel. Change the FPS setting from the default 24 fps to 12 fps.

6. Finally, let's add a code snippet to stop the animation at frame 24 so it doesn't loop. With your cursor on frame 24, open the Code Snippets panel and expand the Timeline Navigation section. Double-click on Stop at this Frame (**Figure 90d**).

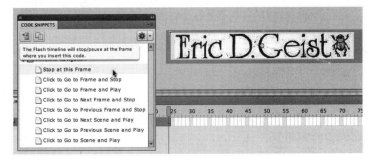

Figure 90d Adding a code snippet to stop an animation.

If You Can Use the Pen Tool...

Designers familiar with the Convert Anchor tool in Illustrator will appreciate that motion tween paths are editable paths. You can use the Convert Anchor Point tool in Flash CS5, which works the same way as its twin in Illustrator CS5. Use the Convert Anchor tool to convert corner anchors to smooth (or combine) anchors.

#91 Generating a Morphing Shape

Multiple Layers?

When you place artwork on different layers in Flash CS5, artwork on layers higher on the list in the Timeline displays on top of artwork on lower layers.

Formatting Type in Flash?

For an exploration of creating and formatting type in Flash CS5 using new typography tools, see #87, "Using the Text Layout Framework (TLF)."

Shape tweening morphs one shape into another. You create one shape in one frame (like the first frame of a movie), another shape in a later frame, and apply shape tweening to generate intermediate shapes—kind of like an animated blend.

As we explore shape tweens, we'll also discuss using more than one layer in a Flash object. In the following How-To, you'll place a shape tween behind static text. You'll be able to easily adapt this to other applications of shape tweens.

1. Create a new Flash file—I'll use a 960-pixel-wide, 100-pixel-high artboard (see 84, "Creating and Exporting Flash Files" for an explanation of how to define Flash artboards).

2. With your cursor in the first frame of the Timeline (the default), create text for your banner.

3. Choose Insert > Timeline > Layer to create a new layer. Double-click on the new layer name in the Timeline, and change it to **Shape Tween**. Double-click on the original layer name, and change it to **Text**. Click and drag on the Text layer to move it to the top of the Timeline (**Figure 91a**).

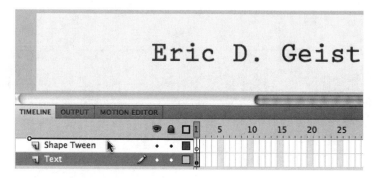

Figure 91a Moving a Timeline layer.

4. Click in the first frame of the Shape Tween layer, and draw a circle, or something close to one.

5. Click on the 48th frame (to allow 2 seconds for the shape tween at the standard animation frame rate of 24 fps). Choose Insert > Timeline > Blank Keyframe. In the 48th frame, draw an elongated oval (**Figure 91b**).

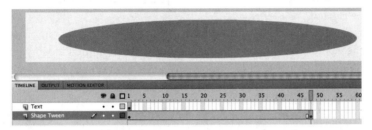

Figure 91b Adding a second shape to prepare a shape tween.

6. Click in any frame between 1 and 47 on the Shape Tween layer, and choose Insert > Shape Tween. A green bar on the Timeline indicates the shape tween has been generated. You can use the scrubber head to preview the shape tweening (**Figure 91c**).

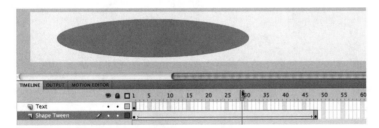

Figure 91c Previewing a shape tween.

7. Finally, extend the Text layer by clicking in frame 48 on the Text layer and choosing Insert > Timeline > Keyframe.

Stop the Movie!

If you want to stop the animation from looping, insert a Stop at this Frame code snippet. For instructions on inserting code snippets, see #89, "Using Code Snippets."

A More Complex Shape Tween?

You can adapt the techniques in #90, "Creating an Animated Movie," to add keyframes, and to edit the shape of the morphing shape tween.

#92 Creating Templates

As you've seen, Flash projects take some time and work. And often you can recycle much of that time and work by opening and modifying already existing files.

To save a Flash file as a template, choose File > Save as Template. Click Save as Template in the warning dialog that tells you the SWF history will be cleared.

In the Save as Template dialog, enter a name for the template in the Name box. Choose a category of template from the Category pop-up menu, and enter a description in the Description box (**Figure 92a**). Click Save.

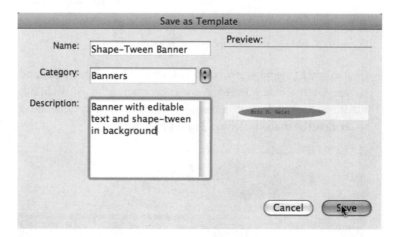

Figure 92a Defining a template.

Creating Flash Professional Web Elements

You can create new Flash files from your template by choosing File > New and selecting the Templates tab in the New dialog. Your custom template will appear in the category you assigned it to (**Figure 92b**).

Saving Template-Generated Files

When you save an edited file created from a template, you'll be prompted to save it as a new Flash (FLA) file.

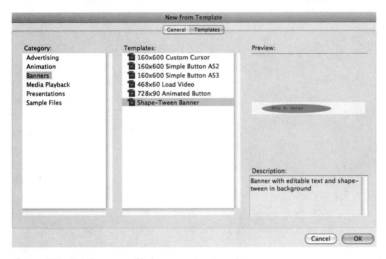

Figure 92b Creating a new file from a custom template.

CHAPTER FOURTEEN

Creating Slideshows in Flash Professional

One of the most frequently asked questions I encounter is: What's the best way to create an attractive slideshow online? Whether you are displaying a portfolio, advertising products, introducing your company or organization, or just sharing a photo album, Flash Professional can create highly inviting presentations.

Flash Professional CS5 comes with templates that simplify and automate creating Flash slideshows. In this chapter, I'll show you how to use them.

In the course of customizing the Flash CS5 Professional Photo Albums, I'll show you techniques for editing templates, actions, and XML code that you can apply to working with other complex Flash interactive objects.

And, at the end of this chapter, I'll address the challenges of making your SWF slideshows accessible in browsing environments that do not support Flash, including Apple iPhones and iPads.

#93 Creating a Simple Photo Album

The "Simple" Photo Album template in Flash Professional CS5 creates a flexible, easy-to-edit presentation that can display photos as a timed slideshow.

Start creating a slideshow by choosing File > New. In the New Document dialog, select the Templates tab. From the Media Playback category, choose Simple Photo Album. The template opens, with a visible instructions layer, and some rather garish default artwork (**Figure 93a**).

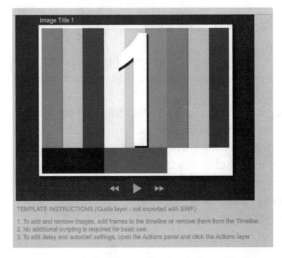

Figure 93a Default settings in the Simple Photo Album template.

Choose File > Save, and save the Flash (FLA) file with any filename.

1. To edit the images and titles for the four default slides, select the first frame in the Images/Titles layer in the Timeline (you may need to expand the Layers area to see the complete Layer title).

2. Double-click on the image title text to select it, and type your own image title.

3. Delete the default image. Copy and paste your own image into the frame. Use the Free Transform tool to edit the image size as needed—hold down the Shift key to maintain height-to-width ratio while resizing (**Figure 93b**). In a similar way, customize the other four default slides.

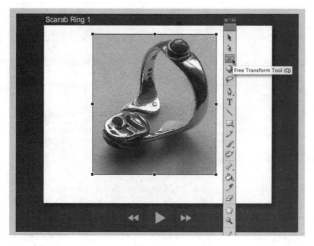

Figure 93b Customizing a slide.

(continued on next page)

Saving to SWF Options... and Other Formats

For an exploration of your options when exporting slideshows for the Web, see #96, "Exporting SWF Slideshows."

Embedding SWFs in Web Pages

You'll find the steps to embed Flash (SWF) files in Web pages in #38, "Embedding Flash (SWF)," in Chapter 6.

Change Timing

You can adjust the timing of the slideshow using the Actions layer and the Actions panel. The process is similar to editing the actions for an Advanced Photo Album. For instructions, see #94, "Creating an Advanced Photo Album."

4. To add a slide, Control+click (Windows) or Command+click (Mac) to select the Controls, Images/Titles, Matte, and Background layers for frame 5, and choose Insert > Timeline > Keyframe (**Figure 93c**). You can repeat these steps in additional frames to add more slides.

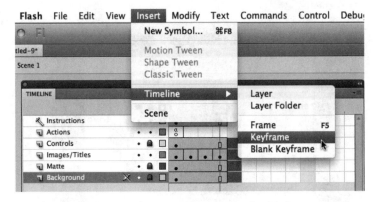

Figure 93c Inserting a new frame to add an image to the slideshow.

To generate a Web-ready SWF that you can embed in Dreamweaver, choose File > Export > Export Movie. There are different export options, but you want to save the slideshow as a SWF file.

#94 Creating an Advanced Photo Album

The Advanced Photo Album converts a set of photos to sized images and thumbnails. It can display a set of photos either as an automatically timed slideshow or as a manual slideshow (the user clicks a thumbnail to see an image). You can define transition effects and timing.

The first step is to collect a set of images. For the purposes of this How-To, we'll work with six images, but you can adjust that to your needs. The Advanced Photo Album will resize both large and thumbnail versions of your image, but I suggest starting with images in the 600-pixel-wide range for best display. Put all your images in a single folder, and rename them **image1.jpg**, **image2.jpg**, and so on (the images must have those exact names).

With your images organized and named, choose File > New. In the New Document dialog, select the Templates tab. From the Media Playback category, choose Advanced Photo Album (**Figure 94a**).

Group Images in Small Sets

I recommend grouping your images in relatively small sets, like six images, for the most effective presentation. More slideshows with smaller sets of images gives the user freedom to view the content he or she wishes to see, and often provides a more powerful, focused presentation.

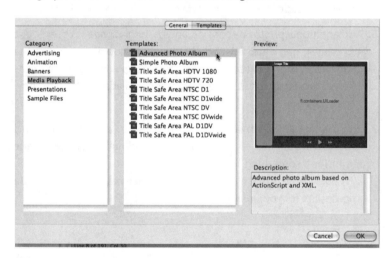

Figure 94a Opening the Advanced Photo Album template.

Choose File > Save, and save the Flash (FLA) file (with any filename) in the same folder you used to store the images you'll use in the slideshow.

Test the slideshow with default settings by choosing Control > Test Movie > in Flash Professional. The slideshow plays with the first four slides only, and with default background, timing, and other settings that you'll adjust in the following steps:

Timelines?

Choose Window > Timeline to display the Timeline if it is not visible. For a survey of how to navigate around the Flash Professional CS5 Timeline, see #88, "Creating a Timeline," in Chapter 13.

Test Anytime!

At any time, while adjusting the slideshow settings, you can test your movie with the current settings. Save the file, and choose Control > Test Movie > in Flash Professional.

1. In the Timeline, select the Actions layer. View the Actions panel (you'll want to make it nice and wide so you can see the code). Scroll through the panel until you find the section `// USER CONFIG SETTINGS =====`.

2. Set the timing of your slideshow by changing the value in the line `var secondsDelay:Number = 2;` to another value (for example, changing 2 to 4 will present each image for 4 seconds).

3. You can turn off autostart (requiring a user to click the Play button to start the show) by changing `var autoStart:Boolean = true;` to `var autoStart:Boolean = false;`.

4. You can turn off transitions by changing `var transitionOn:Boolean = true;` to `var transitionOn:Boolean = false;`.

5. To change the transition effect, substitute one of the listed effects for Fade in the code line `var transitionType:String = "Fade";`.

6. Add additional photos by copying and pasting `<image title='Test 4'>image4.jpg</image>` and changing the copied version of the coding to `<image title='Test 5'>image5.jpg</image>`. Do this as often as necessary for as many images as you placed in the slideshow folder.

7. Edit the Image titles by changing Test 1, Test 2, and so on to actual captions for your images; for example, the coding for your first image might look something like `<image title='scarab'>image1.jpg </image>` (except that instead of scarab you'll have a caption or title appropriate for your image).

Having customized the slideshow content, timing, and effects, a remaining element in creating a customized slideshow is to change the background. The background artwork in this template is somewhat complex, and some of the background elements are essential to the slideshow and cannot easily be edited. But you can change the background color by first unlocking the Background layer (click the lock icon in the layer), selecting the main background rectangle, and assigning a new color in the Properties panel (**Figure 94b**).

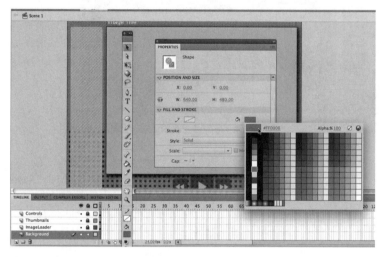

Figure 94b Adjusting the background color of the slideshow.

Dreamweaver Webs?

For instructions on setting up a Dreamweaver Web site, see #1, "Defining a Local Web Site."

Each time you adjust and customize the slideshow, test the presentation (**Figure 94c**).

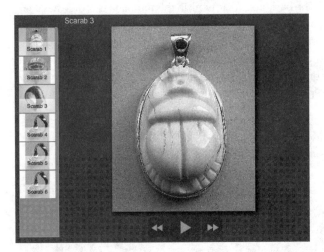

Figure 94c Testing a presentation.

A final but critical step: Choose File > Export > Export Movie. Save the SWF file *in the same folder as the images*. When you embed the slideshow in a Dreamweaver CS5 Web page, copy both the SWF file *and all the images* to the same folder (or subfolder) in the Dreamweaver Web page.

#95 Publishing Slideshows as SWFs

When you publish a slideshow as a SWF, you can choose which version of the Flash Player will be required to play the slideshow. In general, newer versions of the Flash Player support more effects, and publishing to the Flash Player will preserve more controls than publishing to Flash Lite, which is geared to mobile devices. You can also control the quality of embedded JPEG images when you define Publish settings.

Follow these steps to export a Flash (FLA) slideshow to a SWF file, playable on the Web, and an HTML page with the SWF file and player embedded within that page:

1. Access Publish settings by choosing File > Publish Settings. The relevant settings for the Flash slideshows explored in this chapter are in the Flash tab of the Publish Settings dialog.

2. Choose a Player version from the Player pop-up menu.

3. You can reduce file size a bit and not distribute unnecessary information by deselecting the Include Hidden Layers and Include XMP Metadata check boxes. And no other check-box options in this tab are needed—they can all be deselected.

4. Select JPEG quality. The JPEG Quality slider defines the quality (file size) of the JPEG images you embedded in the slideshow. The higher the setting, the better the image quality (but the longer the download time).

(continued on next page)

Which Player Version?

For maximum accessibility, you might choose a Player version one, or even two iterations behind the current version (listed first, and Flash Player 10 at this writing). From the ActionScript pop-up menu, choose the highest version of ActionScript available for the Player you selected in order to preserve the features of your slideshow most accurately. To make the Advanced Photo Album work, you need to save to ActionScript 3.

Generating an HTML Page

You can use the HTML Tab in the Publish Settings dialog to define parameters for an HTML Web page that is generated when you publish your slideshow. This creates a page, with the slideshow in it, that can be opened and edited in Dreamweaver. The Flash Only template works for most situations.

5. Finally, use the Formats tab in the Publish Settings dialog to define the file name and folder to which your files (SWF, and if you choose, HTML) will be saved (**Figure 95a**). Use the blue Select Publish Destination folder icons to define a target folder.

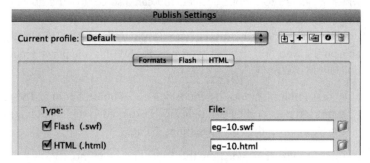

Figure 95a Defining filenames for SWF and HTML files.

6. Choose File > Publish Preview, and choose a format to preview how the published SWF file will look with the settings you selected.

7. To publish all the selected files (in this case, HTML and SWF), choose File > Publish.

#96 Exporting SWF Slideshows

Because Flash is not supported on iPhones, iPads, or in some other mobile environments, you might well want to generate an alternate version of your slideshow for those viewers. You can export the Flash Simple Photo Album explored in this chapter as a QuickTime movie in h.264 format that will play in those devices, and generally the player controls will be supported as well.

The following set of steps will export a slideshow to a QuickTime movie playable on an Apple iPhone 4. You can easily adjust the steps for other environments:

1. With your Flash slideshow file open, choose File > Export Movie. In the Export Movie dialog, navigate to the folder to which you wish to save the slideshow, enter a filename in the Save As box, and choose Quick-Time Movie from the Format pop-up menu.

2. Click Save. The QuickTime Export Settings dialog opens. The default settings export your slideshow just as you defined it, without additional effects or trimming, so there is no need to adjust these. But click the QuickTime settings button. The Movie Settings dialog opens.

(continued on next page)

Exporting to Other Formats?

If you want to export your slideshow to other formats, you can do that in Adobe Media Encoder. First, save the slideshow as a Quick-Time movie, and then convert it to other formats. See #100, "Using Media Encoder," for specific directions.

Filters?

The Movie Settings dialog has a Filters button that allows you to apply Quick-Time filters. You can experiment with filters like Black and White if you wish.

3. In the Video section of the dialog, click the Settings button to open the Standard Video Compression dialog. From the Compression pop-up, choose h.264. This compression setting is widely supported on mobile devices, and particularly promoted by Apple. Leave all the settings at their default values, except that you can adjust the Quality slider in the Compressor section to adjust the quality (and download time) of the exported video. Higher-quality compression takes longer to download but produces better image quality (**Figure 96a**). Click OK in the Standard Video Compression dialog.

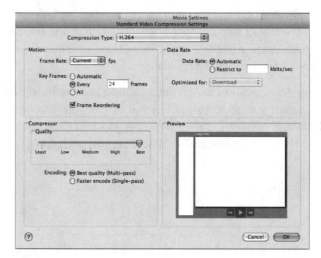

Figure 96a Exporting to the highest-quality h.264 compression video setting.

4. Click the Size button. The Export Size Settings dialog opens. To enter specific values, choose Custom from the Dimensions pop-up menu, and enter values in the two boxes (since many mobile devices can be turned sideways, there is no "height" and "width" box per se). The dimensions for the iPhone 4, for example, are 960 pixels by 640 pixels. Select the Preserve Aspect Ratio Using check box to prevent distortion, and choose either Letterbox (leaving black strips on the top or side as needed) or Crop (cutting off part of the image that doesn't fit in the viewing environment). Click OK in the Export Size settings dialog (**Figure 96b**).

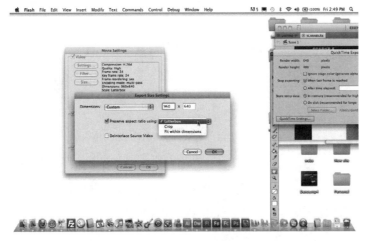

Figure 96b Defining size and letterboxing for a slideshow exported for an iPhone 4.

5. After finalizing your export settings, click OK in the Movie Settings dialog and click the Export button in the QuickTime Export Settings dialog. The resulting h.264 compression QuickTime movie is ready to be embedded in Web pages in Dreamweaver CS5.

CHAPTER FIFTEEN

Using CS5 Tools for the Web

Along with the "big 5" (Dreamweaver, Flash Professional, Flash Catalyst, Illustrator, and Photoshop), Creative Design Suite 5 Web Premium ships with several other major programs: Fireworks, Flash Builder 4 Standard, Contribute, and Acrobat Pro.

Flash Builder Standard is a program for developing "back-end" connections to programs that process data, and is not part of Web "design" per se. Contribute is Adobe's contribution to content management systems (CMSs). This book focuses on working with more widely implemented open source CMSs, like Drupal (see #22, "Connecting Dreamweaver to a CMS Site," and #23, "Formatting CMS Themes," both in Chapter 3). Adobe Acrobat Pro is used to create PDF files.

In addition, Web Premium ships with programs that could be called utilities but are very useful in creating and publishing Web content. We'll focus on those in this chapter. In addition to Device Central (see #8, "Previewing in Live View and Browsers," in Chapter 1), the most valuable (and underrated) utility is Adobe Media Encoder CS5. In a world of fast-changing online video standards, Media Encoder converts video files to a wide range of *other* video formats. We'll also explore Adobe Bridge, which has useful tools for preparing photos for the Web.

While it has not been possible to explore Fireworks in our limited space in this book, in this chapter, I'll show you how to access particularly useful Fireworks features from Bridge.

#97 Managing Files in Bridge

Adobe Bridge serves as kind of a Grand Central Station for coordinating files used in different design projects. Bridge is somewhat tilted toward print design—in part that's because Dreamweaver handles most of the "coordinating" role for Web projects that Bridge plays for print projects. But you can survey more information about your files in Bridge than is easily available through your operating system's file management tools. Photographers use Bridge to batch import, name, and add metadata (like camera information to date).

Bridge is a stand-alone application; you launch it like any other application. It opens with file navigation on the left (viewable in either the Favorites or Folders panel) and a large Preview section in the middle with four views (Essentials, Filmstrip, Metadata, and Output), all of which produce different displays on the right side of the screen. Like other CS5 applications, panels can be viewed or hidden using the Window menu. The Path bar, new to CS5, identifies a breadcrumb-like trail to reveal folder locations in your operating system's file manager.

You can use Adobe Bridge to browse, view, and organize files, but I advise against editing, moving, or renaming files for Web projects in Bridge. Those changes do *not* coordinate with settings in your Dreamweaver CS5 Web, and changing filenames or properties in Bridge can corrupt your Web site (see the "Warning" sidebar).

Although I advise extreme caution in doing any file editing for Web projects in Bridge, there are some tools that can be big timesavers, if applied with care. One is you can rename sets of files. For example, to prepare images for the Flash CS5 Professional Advanced Slideshow template, the images need to be named **image1.jpeg**, **image2.jpeg**, and so on. You can do that renaming in Bridge by following these steps:

Select the files to be renamed in the Content window of Bridge.

1. Choose Tools > Batch Rename from the main Bridge menu.

2. In the Destination Folder area of the Batch Rename dialog, choose an output location. If you select Copy to Another Folder, use the Browse button to locate a new output folder.

3. In the New Filenames area, leave the first pop-up set to Text, the default. Other options allow you to assign attributes like date and time, or file metadata.

Advanced Flash Slideshow

For step-by-step instructions on creating a slideshow using the Flash CS5 Professional Advanced Photo Album, see #94, "Creating an Advanced Photo Album," in Chapter 14.

4. In the next pop-up menu, choose Sequence Number, and enter the number **1** in the next column. Choose One digit from the new pop-up menu that appears.

5. In the third pop-up menu, choose New Extension, and type **JPEG**. I'm doing this because my original filenames use the .jpg filename extension for JPEGs, and the Flash Script requires .jpeg filenames.

6. For the purposes of this recipe, converting the filenames to image1.jpeg, image2.jpeg, and so forth, we do not want any content supplied by the last pop-up, so set it to text and delete any content that appears in the next column (**Figure 97a**). You can preview the output filenames in the New Filename field at the bottom of the window.

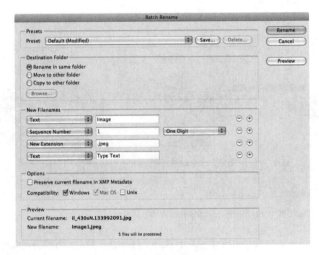

Figure 97a Setting up the Batch Rename dialog to generate new filenames image1.jpeg, image2.jpeg, and so on.

#98 Creating an Adobe Web Gallery

One of the most useful and powerful features of Bridge CS5 for Web designers is the ability to generate a Web gallery. Web galleries (essentially slideshows) are various ways to present sets of images, and all of them work well in Web sites. Bridge CS5 includes some nice new Web Gallery templates, along with the ability to save custom galleries.

To generate a Web gallery, follow these steps:

1. Organize the image files to be included in the gallery in a folder in Bridge.

2. Navigate to the folder with the image files in the Folders panel, and select the Output tab in the top right of the Bridge window (**Figure 98a**).

Figure 98a Selecting files for output to a Web gallery.

3. In the Output panel, click the Web Gallery button. From the Template pop-up menu, choose any of the templates, and choose additional styling from the Style pop-up menu.

4. In the Output panel, expand the Color Palette and Appearance sections. Use the Color Palette swatches to change the color of any element in the gallery, and use the Appearance settings to control display of images. Click the Refresh Preview button to preview the gallery (**Figure 98b**).

Figure 98b Adjusting thumbnail size, and previewing a Web gallery.

5. Expand the Site Info section of the Output tab, and enter content for title, caption, contact information, and so on.

6. Expand the Create Gallery section. If you are saving to a location on your computer, use the Browse button to navigate to and select that location. If you are saving to a remote Web location, enter the FTP connection.

7. After you define output settings, click Save (or Upload to send to a defined remote site). All the files for the Gallery are saved, ready to upload to your Web site in Dreamweaver.

Better to Upload through Dreamweaver

While Adobe Web galleries can be uploaded directly to a remote server using the FTP functions in the Output panel, it's best to manage this file transfer, like all connections between your local and remote Web sites, through Dreamweaver's Files panel. See #2, "Connecting to a Remote Site," and #3, "Managing Sites in the Files Panel," both in Chapter 1. To do this, you should save your Adobe Web gallery to your Dreamweaver Site folder.

Save and Reuse

You can save (and later reuse) custom-defined styles for Web galleries. After you define settings, click the tiny Save Style button just to the right of the Style pop-up. Enter a name in the New Style dialog and click Create. The style will be available from the Style pop-up menu.

#99 Accessing Fireworks from Bridge

Adobe Fireworks CS5 is an illustration and design tool that somewhat straddles the vector/bitmap worlds that are the domain of Illustrator and Photoshop respectively. Bridge provides access to a fairly substantial set of Fireworks features through batch processing—where you select a set of files and apply changes to all of them.

To apply batch processing in Fireworks to a set of images, first select them in the Content tab in Bridge. Then, follow these steps to access different batch-processing options:

1. Choose Tools > Fireworks > Batch. Fireworks CS5 launches, and the Batch Process dialog opens. Your selected files display in the bottom half of the dialog. You can use the Remove button to remove files from the batch set, or select files in the navigation section at the top of the dialog and use the Add or Add All button to include additional files (**Figure 99a**).

Figure 99a Adding files to the queue for batch processing.

Batch Backup

The Incremental Backups option creates copies with a number appended to the end of the filename of the new backup copy. If you deselect the Backups check box, files will be overwritten (unless your batch process involves saving images to a different file format, or to a different folder than the originals).

Other Fireworks Options

You can also convert images to grayscale, sepia, or invert color selection (convert the colors to an inverse value on the 256 color-values scale), or export to FXG format (see the sidebar "FXG Format?") directly from the Tools > Fireworks menu in Bridge.

2. With your set of files selected, click Next. In the new dialog, select different batch options (you can do more than one at a time) from the list on the left of the Batch Process dialog. For example, you can rescale all selected images, sharpen them, and convert them to grayscale; the last two options are available from the expanded Commands list (**Figure 99b**).

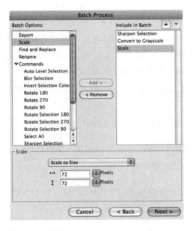

Figure 99b Batch scaling, sharpening, and converting images to grayscale.

3. Click Next. In the final dialog of the Batch wizard, choose an output folder (either the Same Location as the Original File, or use the Browse button to define a Custom Location), and a backup method (see the sidebar "Batch Backup").

4. When you've defined batch settings, click Batch. After the files are processed, they'll be available in the folder you defined for output.

#**100** Using Media Encoder

Support for Many More Formats in CS5

Adobe Media Encoder (formerly Flash Video Encoder) has always been an underrated and valuable tool. In CS5, with the addition of new source-format options (including the ability to convert *from* FLV) and output presets, Media Encoder is an essential element in the toolbox of Web designers.

Formats and Presets?

Video file formats are confusing and, in some ways, deceiving. Different file formats can serve as "shells" for different compression methods (CODECs), while different compression methods (like h.264) can be "housed" in different file formats. Therefore, the actual output of a file is defined as much in the Preset pop-up menu as it is in the Format pop-up, and it is important to make selections from both before converting a video. If you don't see an output format you need in the Preset list, try selecting a different format and see if the target device is listed in the Presets for that format.

Adobe Media Encoder converts just about any media (see the sidebar "Support for Many More Formats in CS5" for exceptions) to any other media—and not just Adobe media files (like Flash SWF or FLV). You can extract a high-quality print still from a video, strip an audio soundtrack out of almost any video file, and batch-convert a video to a dozen other video formats and settings to satisfy viewers in any environment—even Apple iPhones.

As a way of introducing you to Media Encoder's magic in our little bit of remaining space, I'll walk you through a recipe for converting a video from another format (like QuickTime MOV, Windows AVI, or Adobe's Flash Video (FLV) format to an iPhone-ready h.264 video. You'll be able to substitute your own conversion output specs into the recipe to create video for other environments.

Follow these steps to convert a video to an iPhone-ready h.264 file:

1. Launch Media Encoder. This is a stand-alone application that "you can't buy in stores," but it comes with CS5 Web Premium.

2. Click the Add button in the opening dialog. In the Open dialog, navigate to and select video files to convert to another format.

3. For each file you added to the cue, select an output format from the Format pop-up menu. For example, to convert files to the h.264 format promoted by Apple, choose H.264 (**Figure 100a**).

Figure 100a Defining an output format.

4. Next, from the Preset pop-up, choose a format for your output video. The Presets are pretty well labeled, identifying the device (and even the screen orientation) for the output (**Figure 100b**).

Figure 100b Choosing a preset to fit video onto an iPhone viewed widescreen.

5. Click the Ouptut File link. The Save As dialog opens. Navigate to the folder to which you want to save your exported video file, and click Save (clicking Save doesn't actually "save" anything; it just identifies the target folder for what will be a saved, exported video file).

(continued on next page)

Convert to Multiple Formats

It's a multi-video-format world, and you can easily convert a video to many formats so it plays well on an iPod, an iPhone, and a full-sized Windows computer that only plays Windows Media files. To do that, use the Duplicate button in the main Media Encoder window to generate multiple versions of your original file, and then define different output settings for each copy.

Batching

You can batch process video conversions in Media Encoder, and not just similar conversions. Select multiple files by using the Add button repeatedly, or by Shift-clicking on multiple files when you use the Add button. You can line up a set of conversions with different output settings, and then batch process them all at once. Since converting video files from one format to another is resource demanding and takes awhile, you might organize your work to do batch coversion over your lunch or coffee break or even overnight.

Turn Off Autocue

For reasons unfathomable to me, Media Encoder automatically begins batch processing all items added to the queue after 2 minutes, even if you're sitting in front of your computer thinking about what the best possible output format should be. To turn that "feature" off, choose Edit > Preferences (Windows) or Adobe Media Encoder CS5 > Preferences (Mac), and deslect the Start Queue Automatically When Idle For check box.

More Acccessible (Better-Looking?) Interface

I know it's uber-trendy, but I'm not a huge fan of designing interfaces with white type on gray backgrounds. For a more accessible interface look, crank the User Interface Brightness slider in the Preferences dialog all the way up to the right edge of the Lighter scale. I did for the screen captures in this book.

6. After you've defined output settings for one video, or for a set of videos, click Start Cue. Your file(s) will be converted to the selected format(s). You can watch the progress in the area on the bottom of the Media Encoder window (**Figure 100c**).

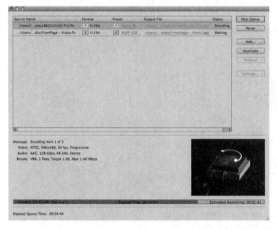

Figure 100c Viewing video conversion progress.

Index